THE
pies and
pastries
COOKBOOK

A SOUTHERN LIVING BOOK

contents

preface

When a *Southern Living* homemaker wants to bring smiles to the faces around her dining table, she features pies and pastries for dessert. Nothing seems to make a mealtime occasion quite so special as do these sweet tooth favorites with their crisp crusts and varied fillings.

Pies and pastries are often one food on which truly great cooks are judged. The crust must be flaky and the filling must not only complement the crust but must be just right — tart or sweet, smooth or crunchy, as called for in the recipe.

In this Southern Living Cookbook Library *Pies and Pastries Cookbook,* hundreds of the very best home-tested recipes from kitchens throughout the Southland have been combined with informative editorial information to make your pies and pastries the best ever. You'll pore through page after page of recipes for fruit pies . . . cream pies . . . custard pies . . . chiffon pies . . . cream puffs and pie shells . . . dumplings and fried pies . . . fritters and turnovers . . . tarts and tassies. There's even a special section devoted to gourmet patisserie — a gourmet's delight of a bake shop that you can create in your own home.

Just-right pies and pastries are yours every time, with the recipes and tips you'll find in this book. From our kitchens to yours, welcome to the wonderful world of pies and pastries — southern style!

A la mode: The term that refers to pie or pastry served with a topping of ice cream.

Apple pie filling: A blend of apple slices, juices, and seasonings sold ready to be used in preparing an apple pie.

Apple pie slices: Apple slices that have been packed in water or light syrup and are ready for mixing with other ingredients to prepare an apple pie filling.

Apple pie spice: A prepared blend of spices called for in many apple pie recipes. Homemakers may create their own apple pie spice by substituting 1/2 tsp. cinnamon, 1/4 tsp. nutmeg, 1/8 tsp. allspice, and 1/8 tsp. cardamom for every teaspoon of spice.

Baba: A light cake made with a yeast dough, raisins, and other dried fruit. After being baked, the cake is soaked in a sweet syrup flavored with liqueurs.

glossary
FOR PIES AND PASTRIES

Babas are popular gourmet pastries.

Cheesecake: A cake baked, like a pie, in a crust. It is made of cheese (cottage or cream); eggs; milk, cream, or sour cream; and flavorings. Recipes will sometimes include fruit or nuts among the ingredients.

Chiffon pie: A pie whose filling has a light and airy texture as a result of the inclusion of partially set gelatin or gelatin and stiffly beaten egg whites with the other ingredients. This filling is turned into baked crusts of crumbs, plain pastry, or meringue, then chilled to set.

Cream pie: Pie in which a prepared filling is placed in a prepared crust. It is assembled rather than baked. In this book, the term also includes frozen pies.

Cream puffs: Pastries made of a hollow shell or puff prepared with pate a choux (see below), and filled with whipped cream or custard. May also be dusted with confectioners' sugar or iced before serving.

Crumb crusts: Pie crusts prepared by mixing cracker or cookie crumbs, sugar, and shortening. The mixture is pressed into a pie plate and baked before being filled.

Crust: The exterior covering of a pie. (See specific type of crust for more detailed information.)

Custard pie: Consists of an egg-based custard filling that is turned into an unbaked pie shell. The entire pie is then baked until the custard is set.

Dumplings: Dessert dumplings feature a fruit center surrounded by dough. When filled, dumpling is dropped into hot liquid and cooked. It may also be baked or steamed.

Fried pies: A fruit or jam filling that is surrounded by pastry and the pie fried in hot fat.

Fritters: From the French *friture*, meaning something fried. A fritter has a fruit center that is dipped in and coated with batter. The pastry is then fried in fat.

Fruit pies: A pie with a fruit-based filling to which either thickened, flavored juice or gelatin has been added. The filling is baked in a shell or between two crusts.

Kuchen: A yeast-based pastry made with cottage cheese, plums, apples, and nuts.

Meringue crusts: Pie crust prepared with a mixture of sugar, stiffly beaten egg whites, cream of tartar, and occasionally, flavoring. Meringue pie crusts are baked and cooled before the filling is added.

Oil pastry: A form of pie crust in which vegetable oil is mixed with flour, salt, and liquid. The vegetable oil replaces the solid shortening used in plain pastry.

Pate a choux: A sweetened pastry dough prepared by mixing flour, water, seasonings, eggs, and butter. The dough is dropped in small amounts onto a baking sheet. As it bakes, it expands, forming hollows that, after baking, may be filled with a sweet mixture (usually whipped cream or custard).

Pie plates: Also known as pie pans, these are round pans with low sides and rims around the edge of the sides. They are most often available in eight- and nine-inch sizes, the size referring to the pan's diameter. Pie plates are made of metal, glass, or enamel. When using the latter two types of pan, reduce oven temperature specified in recipe by 25 degrees.

Plain pastry: A mixture of flour, salt, solid shortening, and liquid. Crusts prepared with this pastry are baked before or after filling, as the recipe specifies.

Pumpkin pie spice: A mixture of spices called for in many pumpkin pie recipes. One teaspoon of this blend is equivalent to 1/2 tsp. cinnamon, 1/4 tsp. ginger, 1/8 tsp. allspice, 1/8 tsp. nutmeg.

Sopaipilla: A Mexican pastry often served as a hot bread with butter or as a dessert with honey, confectioners' sugar, or syrup.

Sour cream: A dairy product prepared by souring cream with cultures. Soured cream is not a substitute.

Streusel: A German pastry topped with a crumb-like mixture of butter, sugar, flour, and cinnamon.

Tart: A small, open faced pastry consisting of a rich pie shell filled with fruit, jam, or custard.

Tassies: Miniature tarts (see above).

Torte: A very rich pastry-like cake made with sugar and eggs and using ground nutmeats (and sometimes bread crumbs) in place of flour. Served iced or with whipped cream.

Turnovers: Small pies made by covering half a piece of plain or puff pastry with a filling, turning the other half over a filling, sealing the edges, and baking the pastry in a hot oven.

Yogurt: A dairy product prepared by souring milk with cultures. Soured milk is not a substitute.

Successful pie and pastry cookery often results from carefully developed recipes prepared by wise homemakers. And many of these same homemakers are quick to admit that a good part of their success is due as much to using the right equipment — and following their own experience-proven tricks — as it is to having a proven recipe. With the equipment suggested below and the hints you'll find in these two pages, successful pies and pastries can be yours, too!

TOOLS FOR SUCCESSFUL PIES AND PASTRIES

There are a few pieces of equipment essential to pie and pastry preparation — and all are inexpensive to purchase and easy to find in local stores. Foremost among the tools you'll want is the *pastry blender*. This utensil has a wooden handle and several thin metal rings which are from one side of the

tips & tools

FOR SUCCESSFUL PASTRIES

handle to the other. When you are preparing pie crust dough, use this blender to cut in shortening with the dry ingredients and to blend water with the shortening-flour mixture. Using a pastry blender is one way to ensure that the tiny particles of shortening — so important in forming a truly flaky crust — don't melt before baking. Cooks who use their hands to cut in shortening and blend water with the dry ingredients often find that the heat of their hands is enough to melt shortening — resulting in tough, unappealing pie crust.

A *cloth covered rolling pin and board* are two more important pieces of equipment. These, too, help ensure a flaky crust. When you are rolling pie crust, if too much flour (used to keep the dough from sticking to either the pin or the rolling surface) gets into the dough it may toughen. But a cloth covering absorbs most of the flour and then releases it a little at a time as it is needed to prevent sticking. You can make your own cloth covering for a rolling pin with a child's white ribbed cotton sock. Cut off the foot portion and discard it. Slip the remaining ribbed part over your rolling pin. And you can create your own cloth board cover, too, with a coarsely textured dish cloth.

To give your pies a professional finished look, consider investing in a *pastry wheel*. This tool cuts out pie crust with a distinctively scalloped edge — giving an attractive look to your lattice-topped pie. A *pastry brush* also lends a professional touch to your pies. Use it to distribute egg white or milk evenly over the top crust for a shiny, appetizing appearance. Finally, *pie tape* helps you avoid the too-browned appearance which often mars the outer rim of pies and pie shells. This tape is wrapped around the outer edge of the pie.

It prevents burning and helps this part of the crust develop the pale golden brown color that is so appetizing to behold.

TIPS FOR SUCCESSFUL PIES AND PASTRIES

For perfectly round pie crusts, form a ball with the dough and flatten it by pressing the side of your hand into it three times in a top-to-bottom direction and three times in a side-to-side direction. Then roll as usual.

To put the top crust onto your pie easily, roll out dough until it is ready to be put on the pie. Cut the slits you want, then pick up one edge of the crust dough on your rolling pin and roll to wrap loosely around the pin. "Unroll" the top layer to form the crust of your pie.

To fit a crumb crust into a 9-inch plate, place the crumb dough into the plate and press down with an 8-inch pie plate. The crust will shape itself between the two plates.

For a non-stick crumb crust, when you're ready to serve your pie, wrap a hot, wet towel around the outside of the pie plate. Hold it there for two or three minutes. Every slice you cut will come out of the pan smoothly and easily.

To save yourself the trouble of thickening juices for fruit pies, substitute tapioca for the flour. Combine the tapioca with the sugar and seasoning you use then add liquid and fruit according to your recipe, turn the mixture into a pie crust and bake. The tapioca thickens the juices during the baking process.

To prevent a soggy bottom crust if your pie has a juicy filling, brush the crust with an egg white or melted butter before adding the filling. And do be sure that the filling is very hot.

When pie juices spill into your oven, sprinkle the spill with salt to prevent smoke and smell.

To avoid spills when you're preparing to bake custard pie, place the shell on your oven rack and pour the filling into it. This avoids the precarious balancing of custard pie as you carry it to the oven.

Prevent ragged edges on your pie meringue when cutting individual slices by dipping the knife you use in warm water. Repeat as often as necessary while you're cutting.

To freeze pies and crusts, remember some hints: Fruit, mince, and chiffon pies freeze well, but custard or meringue ones don't. Freeze a filled pie without wrapping it until it is almost solid — then wrap it, using moisture- and vapor- proof freezer paper. All pies can be frozen for two to three months.

When thawing frozen pie baked before freezing, heat at 350 degrees just until warm. The exception to this rule is chiffon pie which must never be heated. Thaw a chiffon pie in the refrigerator for three hours or at room temperature for 45 minutes.

When thawing a frozen, unbaked pie, cook at the temperature specified in your recipe for the given time plus 15 to 20 minutes.

The central art of making excellent pies and pastries lies in the way you prepare your crust. The finest pie crusts are a delight to the eye as well as the palate. They are pale golden brown, flaky, and are often decorated with cutouts that highlight their appeal.

It's easy to delight your family with such masterpieces of the culinary art. Just remember to follow a few simple rules when you are preparing your pie crust.

MIXING PIE CRUST DOUGH

Flakiness in pie crusts comes from tiny bits of shortening breaking down under intense heat and forming flakes. In mixing your pie crust, be certain that the shortening breaks into bits but doesn't melt. One way to assure this

PREPARING

decorative pastries

is to use a pastry blender, described on page 8. Another is to chill your ingredients *thoroughly*. Chill the water and the shortening. If you're a novice pie crust maker, chill the flour. You might want to chill your pie crust blender, too.

Cut the shortening in lightly but mix enough with the flour to create a blend similar to cornmeal in appearance. Sprinkle the water, a tablespoon at a time, onto the shortening-flour mixture. Mix the liquid and dry ingredients with a tossing motion. Dough is ready for rolling when it cleans the bowl.

ROLLING PIE CRUST DOUGH

The rule for rolling pie crust dough is do it *lightly*. Form dough into a ball and roll from the center of that ball outward. Don't press down hard as you roll. The shortening particles may break down and melt under such pressure. If the dough tears as you roll it, patch it then and there. Tears which go unpatched only get larger. And don't reroll the dough — that's a surefire way to create tough crusts!

When the pie crust has been rolled out, try this easy way to pick it up and fit it into the plate. As shown in the illustration on the previous page, pick up edge of the rolled crust with the rolling pin. Roll the crust *loosely* around the pin, and roll in the opposite direction over the pie plate. The crust will unroll just where you want it. In fitting pie shells into the pan, remember not to stretch the crust or shrinkage will result. In preparing two-crust pies, put the bottom crust into the pan as described, then fill. Put top crust over the filling in the same manner as the bottom crust.

DECORATING PIES AND PASTRIES

Now that you have created a crust certain to be flaky and a delicious filling, what can you do to give it an added decorative zing?

Consider substituting a *lattice top crust* for the more conventional one. Roll the top crust as usual, but cut it into strips about one-half inch in width. Place seven strips, evenly spaced and running in the same direction (either top-to-bottom or side-to-side) across the top of the filling. Weave cross strips until lattice is formed.

A variation of the lattice crust is the *twisted lattice crust*. Cut the strips three-quarters of an inch wide and follow the directions given above for lattice crusts, twisting the lattice strips as you weave them.

Or, give your pastry a *swirled, twisted top crust*. Cut three-quarter inch wide strips of top crust, and moisten the ends. Join the strips to form one long strip. Beginning at the center of the pie, create a swirl with the strip, twisting it as you work.

If a *meringue* pie is going to be your creation, consider the possibilities of a fancy topping. Meringue can be spread and smoothed . . . brought up into decorative peaks . . . or applied with a pastry tube to form fancy shapes.

Dress up open faced pies or tarts with *pastry cutouts*. Roll pastry as for top crust and cut out decorations with cookie cutters. Bake the decorations on a cookie sheet until light brown – use to top pie.

Make the crust which edges your pie an eye-dazzling delight by trimming the crust off at the rim of the pie plate and applying a *decorative edge*. From a long strip of three-quarter-inch wide pastry form your decorative edge. Press one end of the strip to the pastry at the rim of the crust and moisten to hold. Twist the rest of the strip, forming a spiral. Press each open spiral onto the rim.

Using two or three long strands, braid them together. This braid can be used in place of the spiral described above to form a delightful pattern around the edge of your pie.

You can create a *self-edge*, too, if you trim the crust to overlap the plate rim by about one inch. Use this overlap to form delightful designs. Press the crust between your fingers to form a fluted edge. Fold it over, press with the tines of a fork, and you've got a geometric-type design or make scallops by pressing the mouth of a spoon down into the folded dough.

fruit pies

Some of the earliest pies prepared in American kitchens were fruit pies created by thrifty pioneer women who made the most of nature's bounty. Southern homemakers came to judge their pie-making skill on the basis of how well they could prepare succulent fruit pies. Such a tradition was bound to give rise to many delicious recipes — and the very best of these fruit pie recipes are yours now, in this section.

Explore these pages and discover many different ways to prepare that all-American favorite, apple pie. There's a recipe for Apple Crumb Pie, a delicious blend of apple slices, flaky pie crust, and a rich crumbly topping. Another recipe for Apple Cherry Pie combines two tangy fruit flavors in a pie that's as eye-appealing as it is delicious.

Here, too, you'll find recipes long considered a treasured art of southern cookery. Hickory Nut-Grape Pie blends two foods found throughout the Southland into a pie that contrasts flavors and textures in a palate-pleasing manner. Peach Praline Pie features still another mingling of flavors certain to bring you appreciative compliments from friends and family alike. And there is a recipe for Deep Dish Pear Pie, an easy-to-prepare treat that you'll want to serve often.

Why not add a special touch to your next dinner by featuring a fruit pie? You'll be so glad you did!

APPLE CRUMB PIE

4 lge. tart apples	1 tsp. cinnamon
1 unbaked pie shell	3/4 c. flour
1 c. sugar	1/3 c. butter or margarine

Peel the apples and cut into eighths, then arrange in the pie shell. Mix 1/2 cup of the sugar with the cinnamon and sprinkle over the apples. Sift the remaining sugar with the flour, then cut in the butter until crumbly. Sprinkle over the apples. Bake at 400 degrees for 40 to 50 minutes.

Ruby Ray Evans, Post, Texas

APPLE ORCHARD PIE

4 to 6 apples	1 baked pie shell
1/2 c. sugar	1/2 c. heavy cream, whipped
1/4 tsp. nutmeg	1 tbsp. confectioners' sugar

Peel and grate the apples, then add the sugar. Sprinkle with the nutmeg and blend. Turn into the pie shell. Whip the cream until stiff and fold in the confectioners' sugar, then spread over the top of pie. Sprinkle with additional nutmeg.

Mrs. Mary E. Hall, Point Pleasant, West Virginia

MOCK APPLE PIE

36 round buttery crackers	2 tbsp. lemon juice
Pastry for 2-crust pie	Grated rind of 1 lemon
2 c. water	3 tbsp. butter or margarine
2 c. sugar	Cinnamon to taste
2 tsp. cream of tartar	

Break the crackers coarsely into pastry-lined pie pan. Combine the water, sugar and cream of tartar in a saucepan and boil gently for 15 minutes. Add lemon juice and rind, then cool. Pour syrup over crackers. Dot with butter and sprinkle with cinnamon. Cover with the top crust and trim and flute edges together. Cut slits in top crust to allow steam to escape. Bake at 425 degrees for 30 to 35 minutes or until crust is crisp and golden. Serve warm.

Jo Maready, Chinquapin, North Carolina

CHEDDAR APPLE PIE

1 pkg. pie crust mix	2 c. shredded Cheddar cheese
1/2 c. sugar	2 1/2 tbsp. water
1/2 c. (packed) brown sugar	3 lb. apples, sliced
3/4 tsp. cinnamon	1 tbsp. flour
3 tbsp. butter	Nutmeg to taste

Combine 1 cup of the pie crust mix, sugars and cinnamon, then cut in the butter. Set aside. Mix 1 cup of the cheese into remaining pie crust mix, then blend with water. Roll out the dough and line a 9-inch pie plate. Place apples in pastry-lined pie plate. Sprinkle flour evenly through apples, then sprinkle with nutmeg. Cover with half the cinnamon mixture, then sprinkle remaining cheese over all. Top with remaining cinnamon mixture. Bake for about 40 minutes at 375 degrees.

Mrs. Ruth Atkins, Mooresboro, North Carolina

APPLE-ALMOND PIE

8 apples	3 1/2 tbsp. butter or
1/4 c. water	margarine
3/4 c. sugar	1/2 c. sliced almonds
6 1/2 tbsp. flour	

Peel and core the apples, then slice into thin wedges and place in a greased baking dish. Add the water and sprinkle with 1/3 cup sugar. Combine the flour, butter and remaining sugar and mix with a fork until of grainy consistency. Sprinkle over apples, then sprinkle the almonds over the top. Bake at 350 degrees until apples are tender and top is browned.

APPLE PIE

6 apples	1/4 tsp. salt
Pastry for 2-crust pie	1/4 tsp. cinnamon
2 tbsp. flour	1/4 tsp. mace
1 c. sugar	1/2 c. light cream

Peel apples and cut into small pieces. Place in a 9-inch pastry-lined pie pan. Mix the flour, sugar, salt and spices, then sift over the apples. Pour cream over pie. Top with strips of pastry. Bake at 425 degrees for 35 to 40 minutes.

Lillian Bush, Ruleville, Mississippi

CLASSIC APPLE PIE

Pastry for 2-crust pie	1 tbsp. grated lemon peel
3/4 c. sugar	5 c. pared and sliced
1 tbsp. flour	Washington State apples
1/2 tsp. cinnamon	1 tbsp. lemon juice
1/4 tsp. nutmeg	2 tbsp. butter or
1/8 tsp. salt	margarine

Preheat oven to 425 degrees. Roll out half the pastry and line a 9-inch pie plate. Combine the sugar, flour, cinnamon, nutmeg, salt and lemon peel in a bowl, then add the apples and toss to coat evenly. Arrange the apples in the pie plate. Sprinkle with lemon juice and dot with butter. Roll out the remaining pastry and place over apples. Trim pastry rim and flute the edge. Decorate with pastry apples and sprinkle with additional sugar. Prick top with fork. Bake for 40 to 45 minutes.

Photograph for this recipe on page 4.

SHREDDED APPLE PIE

5 med. tart apples	2 tbsp. butter, melted
1 unbaked pie shell	1/2 tsp. cinnamon
1 c. sugar	1/2 c. orange juice
2 tbsp. flour	Juice and grated rind of
1/2 tsp. nutmeg	1/2 lemon

Pare the apples and grate on coarse side of grater, then turn into pie shell. Combine the sugar, flour, nutmeg, butter and cinnamon in a saucepan, then stir in the orange and lemon juices and grated rind. Simmer, stirring until sugar is dissolved. Cool slightly, then pour over the apples.

Topping

1/2 c. sugar	3/4 c. flour
1/3 c. chopped pecans	1/3 c. butter or margarine

Combine the sugar, pecans and flour, then cut in the butter until crumbly. Sprinkle over apples. Bake at 400 degrees for 5 minutes, then reduce the oven temperature to 350 degrees and bake for 30 minutes longer or until done. Cool. Garnish with whipped cream and cinnamon-sugar before serving.

Mrs. Ted Beckwith, Nashville, Tennessee

GREEN APPLE CRISP

3 c. sliced green apples	1/4 tsp. salt
3/4 c. sugar	1/2 tsp. cinnamon
3/4 c. flour	1/2 c. soft butter

Arrange apples in a greased baking dish and sprinkle with 1 tablespoon sugar. Combine flour, salt, cinnamon, remaining sugar and butter and mix until crumbly. Sprinkle over apples. Bake at 375 degrees until brown and crisp. Serve warm.

Mrs. Robert W. Russell, Albemarle, North Carolina

OLD-FASHIONED APPLE PIE

1 recipe pastry for	1/2 tsp. cinnamon
2-crust pie	1 tbsp. cornstarch
4 c. sliced fresh apples	Juice and grated rind
1 c. sugar	of 1 lemon
1/4 tsp. nutmeg	3 tbsp. butter

Line a deep 9-inch pie pan with half the pastry. Combine the apples, sugar, nutmeg, cinnamon, cornstarch, lemon juice and rind and mix well. Turn into the pastry-lined pan and dot with the butter. Cover with the remaining pastry, then trim edges and flute. Cut slits for steam to escape. Bake at 375 degrees for 10 minutes, then reduce temperature to 300 degrees. Bake for 30 minutes longer or until pastry is brown and apples are tender. Serve with cheese wedges.

WALNUT CRUMB APPLE PIE

1 1/2 tbsp. quick-cooking tapioca	3/4 tsp. cinnamon
	1/4 tsp. nutmeg
3/4 c. sugar	2 1/2 c. sliced pie apples
1/8 tsp. salt	1 pie shell

Combine the tapioca, sugar, salt, spices and apples, then turn into the pie shell. Bake at 425 degrees for 30 minutes.

Walnut Crumb Topping

1/2 c. sugar	1/4 c. chopped walnuts
1/2 c. fine graham cracker crumbs	1 tsp. cinnamon
	1/8 tsp. salt
1/4 c. flour	1/2 c. melted butter

Combine all the ingredients except the butter. Remove the pie from oven and sprinkle with the crumb mixture. Spoon the butter over the crumb mixture and return to the oven. Bake for 20 minutes longer.

Diane Dick, Eubank, Kentucky

DUTCH APPLE PIE

1 c. sugar	1/2 c. flour
1 tbsp. cinnamon	1/3 c. butter
4 tart apples, sliced	3 or 4 tbsp. orange juice
1 unbaked pie shell	

Combine 1/2 cup sugar and cinnamon, then mix with the apples. Place in the pie shell. Sift the remaining sugar and flour in a bowl and cut in butter until crumbly. Sprinkle crumbs over pie, then drizzle orange juice over crumbs. Bake at 450 degrees for 15 minutes, then reduce oven temperature to 350 degrees and bake for about 45 minutes longer.

Mrs. C. H. White, Chattanooga, Tennessee

VERY BEST APPLE PIE

Pastry for 2-crust pie	1 c. sugar
1 tbsp. flour	3/4 c. orange juice
4 tbsp. melted butter	3 Winesap apples, sliced
1 tsp. nutmeg	

Chill the pastry for 2 hours. Mix the flour and butter in a saucepan, then add the nutmeg, sugar and orange juice and mix well. Simmer, stirring, until sugar is dissolved. Place apples in pastry-lined pie pan, then pour the sugar mixture over the apples. Arrange pastry strips over apples in lattice fashion. Bake in 350-degree oven for 15 minutes. Reduce oven temperature to 300 degrees and bake for about 25 to 30 minutes longer.

Mrs. R. T. De Marcus, Knoxville, Tennessee

BEST APPLE COBBLER

3 c. biscuit mix	Juice of 1 orange
1/4 c. sugar	6 lge. green apples
1/2 c. light cream	Cinnamon to taste

Combine the biscuit mix, sugar, cream and orange juice in a mixing bowl and stir until dough leaves side of bowl. Knead several times on lightly floured board. Roll out about 3/4 of the dough on lightly floured board to a 9 x 13-inch rectangle, 1/4 inch thick. Place in baking dish. Slice the apples into thin wedges and arrange over the dough. Sprinkle with cinnamon and additional sugar. Roll out the remaining dough and cut into thin strips. Arrange in crisscross fashion over apples. Bake at 375 degrees for 25 to 30 minutes or until browned and apples are tender.

TOPSY-TURVY APPLE PIE

2 tbsp. soft butter	3/4 c. sugar
30 pecan halves	2 tbsp. flour
1/3 c. (packed) brown sugar	1 tbsp. cinnamon
Pastry for 2-crust pie	1/2 tsp. nutmeg
6 c. sliced apples	2 tbsp. evaporated milk

Preheat oven to 450 degrees. Line a 9-inch pie pan with foil, leaving 1 inch hanging over edge. Spread butter over side and bottom of foil, then place pecan halves over bottom and side of foil. Sprinkle the brown sugar over pecans and pat into the butter. Roll out half the pastry to fit pan then place over the pecans. Mix the apples, sugar, flour, cinnamon and nutmeg and turn into pastry-lined pan. Cover with remaining pastry, then prick with fork to allow steam to escape. Brush with milk. Bake for 10 minutes, then reduce temperature to 375 degrees and bake for 35 to 40 minutes longer. Invert on serving plate and serve warm.

Mrs. Hubert Miers, West Palm Beach, Florida

APPLE-CHERRY PIE

2 c. flour	2/3 c. shortening
1 tsp. salt	6 to 7 tbsp. cold water

Sift the flour and salt into mixing bowl, then cut in shortening until particles are size of peas. Sprinkle cold water over flour mixture and toss until mixture holds together. Divide dough in half and shape into balls. Roll out half the dough on floured surface to 1 1/2 inches larger than pie pan. Fit loosely into pie pan.

Filling

1 can sour pie cherries	1/4 tsp. salt
1 c. pared and sliced apples	1/4 tsp. nutmeg
1 c. sugar	3 tbsp. quick-cooking tapioca
1/4 c. (packed) brown sugar	2 drops of red food coloring
1/2 tsp. cinnamon	2 tbsp. butter

Combine all the ingredients except the butter in a mixing bowl and mix well. Let stand for 15 minutes. Turn into pastry-lined pan and dot with the butter. Roll out remaining dough and cut slits for steam to escape. Moisten rim of bottom crust and place top crust over filling. Fold edge under bottom crust. Press to seal, then flute. Bake at 450 degrees for 10 minutes, then reduce oven temperature to 375 degrees and bake for 40 to 45 minutes longer.

Mrs. Ed. Steinke, Birmingham, Alabama

CIRCUS PIE

1 can sliced apples	2 tbsp. flour
1 can crushed pineapple	1/4 tsp. cinnamon

1 tsp. lemon juice
1 1/2 c. sugar
Pastry for 1-crust pie

1 tsp. grated lemon rind
Butter
Cherries

Drain the juice from the apples and pineapple into a saucepan, then add the flour, cinnamon and lemon juice. Simmer, stirring constantly, until thickened. Combine apples and pineapple with sugar. Place in pastry-lined pie pan. Add the lemon rind to the juice mixture and cool. Pour into pie shell. Dot with butter. Cut 3 rings with doughnut cutter from remaining pastry. Arrange rings on pie and place cherries in holes. Bake at 375 degrees for about 40 minutes or until crust is brown.

Mrs. Lee Stringfield, Sr., Cottageville, South Carolina

BLUEBERRY PIE WITH RELISH

1 pkg. pie crust mix
2 c. fresh blueberries
1   14-oz. jar cranberry-orange
    relish

2 tbsp. cornstarch
1/3 c. (packed) light
    brown sugar
1/2 c. chopped nuts

Preheat oven to 375 degrees. Prepare the pie crust mix according to package directions. Roll out 1/2 of the pastry and line the bottom and side of an ungreased 9-inch pie pan. Rinse the blueberries and drain, then add the remaining ingredients and blend well. Fill the pastry-lined pie pan with the blueberry mixture. Roll out the remaining pastry and cover top of pie. Seal the edges together with water, then flute. Prick the top to allow steam to escape. Bake for 35 to 40 minutes or until top is light brown. Cool thoroughly before cutting. May use 1 can blueberry pie filling and eliminate cornstarch and sugar, if desired.

FRESH BLACKBERRY PIE

2 1/2 tbsp. cornstarch	Pastry for 2-crust pie
1 c. sugar	Margarine
4 c. fresh blackberries	

Combine the cornstarch with the sugar and mix well, then stir into the blackberries. Pour into pastry-lined pan and dot with margarine. Cover with top crust and vent top with several slashes. Seal and flute edges. Bake at 425 degrees for 35 to 45 minutes or until crust is brown. Cool. Blueberries, raspberries or strawberries may be substituted for blackberries.

Phyllis Thomas, Foreman, Arkansas

BOYSENBERRY PETAL PIE

2 1-lb. 1-oz. jars boysenberries	1/4 tsp. cinnamon
2 tbsp. sugar	Pastry for 2-crust pie
1/4 c. cornstarch	1 tbsp. butter

Drain the boysenberries and reserve 2 cups juice. Combine the sugar, cornstarch and cinnamon in a saucepan and stir in reserved juice slowly. Cook over medium heat, stirring, until thickened. Cool, then add the boysenberries. Pour into pie shell and dot with butter. Place top crust over filling. Bake in 425-degree oven for about 40 minutes.

Mrs. G. L. Brown, Austin, Texas

ROYAL HAWAIIAN BANANA PIE

5 or 6 bananas	1/2 c. sugar
1/2 c. pineapple juice	1 tsp. cinnamon
Pastry for 2-crust pie	2 tbsp. butter

Slice the bananas and cover with the pineapple juice, then toss gently until slices are coated. Let set for 30 minutes and drain. Place bananas in pastry-lined pie pan. Mix the sugar and cinnamon and sift over the bananas. Dot with butter. Place top crust over bananas and seal edges. Vent top with 2 or 3 slashes near center. Bake at 400 degrees for about 30 minutes or until crust is golden brown. Serve hot or cold.

Nancy Vecera, Bellaire, Texas

BANANA-BLUEBERRY PIE

1 No. 303 can blueberries	2 or 3 bananas
3/4 c. sugar	1 baked pie shell
3 tbsp. flour	Whipped cream
Dash of salt	

Drain the blueberries and reserve the juice. Combine the reserved juice with the sugar, flour and salt in a saucepan and cook, stirring, until thick. Add the blueberries and cool. Slice the bananas into the pie shell, then add the blueberry mixture. Top with whipped cream.

Mrs. H. D. Griggs, Shawnee, Oklahoma

BLUEBERRY PIE

1 pt. blueberries	1 egg, beaten
1 unbaked pie shell	3/4 c. flour
1/4 c. butter	1 tsp. vanilla
1 c. sugar	

Wash the blueberries and place in pie shell. Cream the butter and sugar in a bowl. Add the egg, flour and vanilla and mix well. Spread on blueberries. Bake at 350 degrees for about 50 minutes or until done.

Glennie Haskins, Trenton, North Carolina

OLD-FASHIONED BLUEBERRY SPOON PIE

2 1-lb. 6-oz. cans	2 tbsp. butter or
blueberry pie filling	margarine
Grated rind of 1 orange	1 pkg. pie crust mix
1 tsp. ground nutmeg	

Preheat oven to 375 degrees. Mix the pie filling, orange rind and nutmeg and pour into a 1 1/2-quart casserole. Dot top with butter. Prepare the pie crust mix according to package directions and roll out on a lightly floured board to a 10-inch circle. Cut pastry with a sharp knife into 1/2-inch wide strips. Arrange strips over blueberry filling in a lattice pattern. Place remaining strips around outer rim of pie. Bake for 20 to 25 minutes until crust is golden brown and filling is bubbly. Spoon into individual dessert bowls and top with thick cream or whipped cream, if desired.

CHERRY GELATIN PIE

1 can tart cherries	1 sm. box cherry gelatin
1 c. sugar	1 graham cracker crust

Place the undrained cherries and sugar in a saucepan and bring to a boil, stirring constantly. Stir in the gelatin until dissolved, then chill until partially set. Place in the graham cracker crust and chill overnight.

Mrs. S. C. Sprewell, Thorsby, Alabama

CHERRY PIE

2 1/2 c. sour cherries	3 tbsp. tapioca
1/3 c. cherry juice	1/8 tsp. almond extract (opt.)
1/3 c. (packed) brown sugar	Pastry for 2-crust pie
1/3 c. sugar	1 tbsp. butter

Combine the cherries, juice, sugars, tapioca and extract in a bowl and let stand for 15 minutes. Pour into pastry-lined pie plate and dot with butter. Cover with top crust and vent with several cuts in center. Bake at 425 degrees for 10 minutes. Reduce temperature to 375 degrees and bake for 30 minutes longer.

Mary Stoltzfus, Grayson, North Carolina

CHERRY-PEACH PIE

1/3 c. melted butter or margarine	3 tbsp. light brown sugar
2 c. gingersnap crumbs	Dash of cinnamon
1 8-oz. jar maraschino cherries	Dash of allspice
2 tbsp. cornstarch	3 tbsp. lemon juice
	6 c. sliced peaches
	2 c. sweetened whipped cream

Mix the butter with crumbs and press over bottom and side of a 9-inch pie pan. Chill. Drain the cherries and reserve syrup. Cut the cherries in half. Add enough water to reserved syrup to make 1/2 cup liquid. Mix the cornstarch, sugar and spices in a saucepan and stir in the liquid and lemon juice. Bring to a boil, stirring constantly, and boil for 30 seconds. Stir in the cherries and cool. Stir in the peaches and turn into pie shell. Chill. Top with whipped cream just before serving.

Mrs. Dewey Cline, Whittier, North Carolina

GOOSEBERRY PIE

1 5/8 c. flour	1 tbsp. cornstarch
1/2 c. butter or margarine	1 qt. gooseberries
3 tbsp. water or cream	Cheese slices
6 tbsp. sugar	

Place the flour in a bowl and cut in the butter until of cornmeal consistency. Blend in the water until the dough clings together. Chill the dough thoroughly. Roll out 1/2 of the dough and place in a 10-inch pie pan. Trim the edge carefully. Roll out the remaining dough and cut ten 2-inch squares and one 4-inch star. Arrange the squares to extend 2 inches over edge of pie pan with points toward center. Combine the sugar and cornstarch, then layer the gooseberries and sugar mixture in the pie shell. Fold the pastry wedges over top, then arrange the star in center. Bake at 400 degrees for about 30 minutes or until pastry is browned. Cut 10 cheese triangles and 1 cheese star and arrange over pastry. Return to oven and bake until cheese is melted.

Photograph for this recipe on page 12.

GRAPE-ORANGE PIE

1 1/2 c. graham cracker crumbs	2 c. whipped cream
1/2 c. sugar	3 navel oranges
1/2 c. melted butter	1 sm. jar red currant jelly
1 pkg. lemon gelatin	1 c. chopped almonds
1 8-oz. package cream cheese	1 c. halved green grapes

Combine the crumbs, 1/4 cup sugar and butter and mix well. Press to bottom and half way up side of 10-inch glass baking dish. Chill thoroughly. Dissolve the gelatin and remaining sugar in 1 cup boiling water. Chill until thickened. Blend the cream cheese until smooth, then combine with the gelatin, mixing well. Fold in the whipped cream and turn into the crust. Chill for 2 hours. Peel and slice the oranges crosswise. Melt the jelly in an 8-inch skillet, then add the orange slices, turning to coat both sides. Let stand for 15 minutes. Arrange the oranges over the filling and drizzle any remaining jelly over top. Sprinkle the almonds around the edge. Arrange the grape halves around edge of pie. Garnish top with whole grapes. Chill until serving time.

HICKORY NUT-GRAPE PIE

1 1/2 qt. stemmed grapes	1/8 tsp. salt
1 1/2 c. sugar	1/2 c. chopped hickory nuts
3 tbsp. quick-cooking tapioca	Pastry for 2-crust pie
1 tsp. butter	

Wash the grapes. Remove pulp from skins and reserve skins. Place the pulp in a saucepan and bring to a boil. Press through a sieve to remove seeds. Add enough pulp to skins to make 3 1/2 cups grapes. Add the sugar, tapioca, butter, salt and hickory nuts and mix well. Pour into pie shell and cover with pastry. Cut slits in top crust. Bake at 425 degrees for 15 minutes. Reduce temperature to 400 degrees and bake for 30 minutes longer or until brown.

Mrs. Virginia Fulton, Charlotte, North Carolina

CANNED PEACH PIE

1 recipe pie pastry	2 tbsp. cornstarch
1 lge. can peach halves	1 c. water
1 tbsp. butter	1/2 pt. whipping cream,
Grated rind and juice of	whipped
1 lemon	Rum to taste

Line a deep pie pan with pastry. Bake at 425 degrees until brown. Drain the peaches and reserve syrup. Place reserved syrup, butter, lemon rind and juice in a saucepan. Mix the cornstarch with water and stir into the lemon mixture. Cook until thick, stirring constantly. Cool. Place the peaches in pie crust and pour lemon mixture over peaches. Mix the whipped cream with rum. Place over peaches and garnish with maraschino cherries.

Mrs. William K. Morton, Bon Air, Virginia

FRESH PEACH COBBLER

2 3/4 c. flour	2/3 c. shortening
1 c. sugar	1/3 c. cold water
4 c. sliced fresh peaches	Butter
1 tsp. salt	

Mix 1/4 cup flour and sugar in a saucepan. Add peaches and mix. Bring to a boil and reduce heat. Simmer for 10 to 15 minutes or until peaches are tender. Remove from heat and cool. Mix remaining flour and salt in a bowl and cut in the shortening. Add the water and mix well. Let stand for several minutes. Roll out 1/3 of the pastry as for pie crust to fit bottom of a shallow baking dish. Place on a cookie sheet. Bake at 400 degrees until golden brown. Place in the baking dish. Pour peach mixture over pastry and dot with butter. Roll out remaining pastry and cut into strips. Place over peaches. Bake until golden brown. Serve with whipped cream or ice cream, if desired. Frozen peaches may be substituted for fresh peaches, omitting sugar.

Mrs. C. W. Bibb, Guntersville, Alabama

CREAM-KIST PEACH PIE

6 to 8 fresh peaches, halved	1/8 tsp. salt
1 unbaked pie shell	1/4 tsp. nutmeg
1/2 c. sugar	1/2 tsp. vanilla
2 tbsp. flour	1/2 c. heavy cream
	3 tbsp. chopped almonds

Arrange the peach halves in the pie shell, cut side up. Combine the sugar, flour, salt, nutmeg, vanilla and cream and pour over peaches. Sprinkle with almonds. Bake in 400-degree oven for 45 to 55 minutes. Serve warm.

Mrs. Jack Bether, Lancaster, South Carolina

TEMPTING PEACH PIE

5 c. peeled sliced fresh peaches	1 tsp. vanilla
2 tbsp. cornstarch	Pastry for 2-crust pie
3/4 c. sugar	2 tbsp. butter or margarine
1/4 tsp. salt	

Combine the peaches, cornstarch, sugar, salt and vanilla. Roll out half the pastry 1/8 inch thick and place in a 9-inch pie pan. Add the peach mixture and dot with butter. Roll out the remaining pastry 1/8 inch thick into a 5 x 10-inch rectangle, then cut into ten 1/2-inch wide strips. Arrange lattice-fashion over pie. Trim, turn under and flute edge. Bake in 425-degree oven for 15 minutes. Reduce temperature to 375 degrees and bake for 30 minutes longer or until crust is brown and peaches are tender. Cool.

PEACH PRALINE PIE

4 c. peeled sliced peaches	1/4 c. (firmly packed) brown
3/4 c. sugar	sugar
2 tbsp. quick-cooking	1/4 c. butter or margarine
tapioca	1/2 c. chopped pecans
1/2 c. sifted flour	1 unbaked 9-in. pastry shell

Mix the peaches, sugar and tapioca in a large bowl and let stand for several minutes. Combine the flour and brown sugar in a small bowl and cut in butter until mixture is crumbly. Stir in pecans. Sprinkle 1/3 of the mixture over pastry shell and top with peach mixture. Sprinkle with remaining pecan mixture. Bake at 450 degrees for 10 minutes. Reduce temperature to 350 degrees and bake for 20 minutes longer or until peaches are tender and topping is golden. Cool on wire rack.

Mrs. B. P. Eichelberger, Albertville, Alabama

SKILLET PEACH PIE

2 c. flour	6 to 8 fresh peaches, sliced
1 1/2 tsp. salt	3/4 c. sugar
4 tsp. baking powder	1/2 tsp. cinnamon
6 tbsp. shortening	2 tbsp. butter
1/2 to 2/3 c. milk	

Sift the flour with 1 teaspoon salt and baking powder into a mixing bowl and cut in shortening. Add enough milk to make a soft dough and mix well. Knead lightly on a floured surface and roll out 1/8 inch thick. Place in a heavy 10-inch skillet, letting dough hang over edge. Add the peaches and sprinkle with sugar, remaining salt and cinnamon. Dot with butter. Fold extra dough toward center, leaving center uncovered. Bake at 450 degrees for 10 minutes. Reduce temperature to 375 degrees and bake for 25 to 30 minutes longer. Serve warm with whipped cream, if desired. Four cups sliced canned peaches and 1/4 cup sugar may be substituted for fresh peaches. 6-8 servings.

Mrs. Olen Simpson, Winslow, Arkansas

HOLIDAY MINCEMEAT PIE

1 28-oz. jar mincemeat	2 tbsp. flour
1 unbaked 9-in. pastry shell	1 c. heavy cream
3 tbsp. brown sugar	3/4 c. chopped pecans

Spread the mincemeat in pastry shell. Combine the brown sugar and flour and stir in heavy cream. Pour over mincemeat and sprinkle with pecans. Bake at 425 degrees for 40 to 45 minutes.

Mrs. M. S. Gross, Birmingham, Alabama

OLD-FASHIONED MINCE PIE

3 c. mincemeat   Pastry for 2-crust pie
1 1/2 c. chopped apples

Mix the mincemeat and apples and place in pastry shell. Cover with top crust and cut slits in center. Bake in 425-degree oven for 40 to 45 minutes or until brown. Serve warm.

Mrs. Geraldine Mars, Iuka, Mississippi

COMPANY FRUIT PIE

3 lge. cooking apples	1 tsp. grated lemon rind
3/4 c. golden seedless	1 tsp. grated orange rind
raisins	2 tbsp. lemon juice
1/3 c. currants	1/2 c. orange juice
1/3 c. dried apricots	1/3 c. California sherry
1/3 c. grated citron	1 tbsp. cornstarch
1/4 tsp. salt	2/3 c. sugar
1/2 tsp. cinnamon	2 tbsp. butter or margarine
1/4 tsp. cloves	Pastry for 2-crust 9-in. pie

Pare, core and dice the apples. Rinse and drain the raisins, currants and apricots, then slice the apricots. Combine the dried fruits, apples, citron, salt, spices, rinds, juices and sherry in a saucepan and simmer for 15 minutes or until apples are almost tender. Blend cornstarch and sugar and stir into the fruit mixture. Cook, stirring, until clear and slightly thickened. Add the butter. Cool slightly. Turn the fruit mixture into a pastry-lined pie pan and cover with the top pastry, pinching the edges together firmly to seal. Cut 6 small triangles in pastry and fold back for steam vents. Bake at 425 degrees for about 15 to 30 minutes.

DEEP-DISH PEAR PIE

1 c. sifted all-purpose	1/3 c. shortening
flour	1/4 c. grated Cheddar cheese
1/2 tsp. salt	2 to 3 tbsp. cold water

Sift the flour and salt together into a bowl and cut in shortening until mixture resembles coarse cornmeal. Stir in the cheese. Add the water, 1 tablespoon at time, mixing just until flour is moistened. Chill.

Pear Filling

2 lb. pears	1/2 tsp. cinnamon
2 tbsp. lemon juice	1/2 tsp. nutmeg
3 tbsp. flour	2 tbsp. butter or
1 c. sugar	margarine
Dash of salt	

Peel the pears, cut in halves and core. Arrange in a 1 1/2-quart baking dish and sprinkle with lemon juice. Mix the flour, sugar, salt, cinnamon and nutmeg and sprinkle over pears. Dot with butter. Roll out pastry on a floured surface into a circle a little larger than top of baking dish. Slash in several places in the center and arrange over pears, crimping to edges of dish securely. Bake at 350 degrees for 30 to 40 minutes. Serve with cream, if desired. 6 servings.

Cathleen Adams, LaFayette, Alabama

FRESH PLUM PIE

2 lb. fresh plums	2 tbsp. flour
Pastry for 2-crust pie	1/2 tsp. cinnamon
3/4 c. sugar	1 tbsp. butter

Wash the plums, cut in halves and remove pits. Arrange plums in pie shell. Blend the sugar with flour and cinnamon and sprinkle over plums. Dot with butter. Cover with pastry and slit in several places. Flute edge. Bake at 450 degrees for 12 minutes. Reduce temperature to 325 degrees and bake for 25 minutes longer or until plums are tender. Remove to rack to cool.

Mary Sue Shedrich, Edison, Georgia

ELEGANT RHUBARB PIE

1 3/4 lb. rhubarb	2 tbsp. melted butter or
1 1/2 c. sugar	margarine
2 tbsp. flour	1 egg, slightly beaten
1/4 tsp. salt	Pastry for 2-crust pie

Cut the rhubarb into 1-inch pieces. Mix the sugar, flour, salt, butter and egg in a bowl until well blended. Place the rhubarb in pastry-lined pie plate and spread sugar mixture over rhubarb. Cover with slashed top crust and flute edge. Bake at 425 degrees for about 40 minutes.

Margaret Walker, Manchester, Kentucky

FRESH PINEAPPLE PIE

1 fresh pineapple, diced	1 baked pastry shell
1 c. sugar	1/2 pt. whipping cream,
1/4 c. cornstarch	whipped
1/4 tsp. salt	

Place the pineapple in a bowl and cover with sugar. Let stand overnight. Drain the pineapple and reserve juice. Add enough water to reserved juice to make 1 1/2 cups liquid. Combine cornstarch and salt in a saucepan and add enough pineapple liquid to make a smooth paste. Add remaining liquid. Bring to a boil and cook until clear, stirring frequently. Add the pineapple and cool. Pour into pie shell. Place whipped cream on top.

Mrs. J. W. Mills, Falls Church, Virginia

MINCED CRANBERRY PIE

3 c. fresh cranberries	1 1/4 c. sugar
2 c. chopped tart apples	1/2 tsp. cinnamon
1/4 c. currants	1/2 tsp. mace
1/2 c. raisins	1/2 tsp. cloves
1/4 c. chopped suet	1/4 tsp. salt
1/4 c. finely cut citron	1/2 c. cider
1 tbsp. grated orange rind	1/3 c. dark rum (opt.)
1/4 c. molasses	Pastry for 2-crust pie

Rinse and drain the cranberries. Combine all the ingredients except the rum and pastry. Bring just to a boil, then cover and simmer for 30 minutes. Cool, then add the rum and mix well. Line a 9-inch pie pan with half the pastry. Pour in the cranberry filling and cover with the top crust. Flute the edge and cut several slits in top crust. Place a 2-inch strip of foil around rim of pie to prevent overbrowning. Place pie on lowest shelf of oven. Bake at 425 degrees for 50 to 55 minutes. Remove foil last 5 minutes. Serve warm.

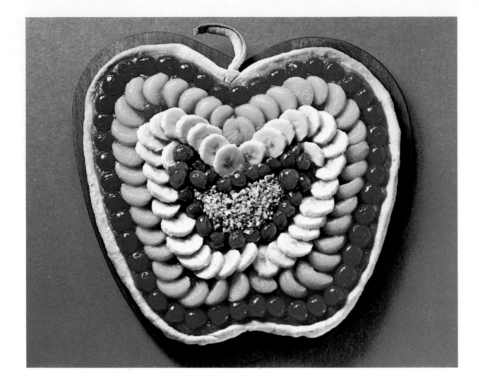

FRUIT-APPLESAUCE PIE

1   10-oz. package pie crust
      mix
4 c. canned applesauce
1 c. (packed) brown sugar
1 tbsp. vinegar
3 tbsp. lemon juice
1 tsp. cinnamon
1/2 tsp. ground cloves
1/4 tsp. allspice

1/4 tsp. salt
1 c. red maraschino cherries
1/2 c. green maraschino
      cherries
1 c. mandarin oranges
2 lge. bananas, sliced
1/4 c. chopped pecans or
      walnuts

Prepare the pie crust mix according to directions. Draw an outline of a large
apple, about 15 inches wide and 13 inches high. Trace on cardboard and cut out.
Cover both sides with several layers of aluminum foil. Roll out the pastry 1/2
inch larger than apple pattern. Fold excess pastry to make a standing edge
around outer rim of the apple. Prick the pastry with a fork. Bake in 425-degree
oven for 20 minutes. Cool. Combine the applesauce, brown sugar, vinegar, 1
tablespoon lemon juice, spices and salt in a 3-quart saucepan. Simmer, stirring
occasionally, for 1 hour. Remove from heat and chill thoroughly. Drain the
cherries and cut in half. Drain the oranges. Place the fruits on layers of paper
toweling to remove excess moisture. Place banana slices in bowl and sprinkle
with the remaining lemon juice. Place the crust on a large platter or bread board.
Spread with 1 1/2 cups of the chilled applesauce mixture. Arrange the red maraschino cherries at outer edge, cut side down. Add the orange sections, bananas,
green cherries and pecans. Cut in wedges to serve. Top with whipped cream,
frozen whipped topping or ice cream, if desired. 10-12 servings.

STRAWBERRY PIE

1 5/8 c. flour	3 tbsp. sugar
1/2 c. butter or margarine	1 tbsp. cornstarch
3 tbsp. cream or water	1 egg, beaten
1 qt. strawberries	

Place the flour in a bowl and cut in the butter until of cornmeal consistency. Blend in the cream until dough clings together. Chill the dough thoroughly. Roll out half the dough on a floured surface and place in a 9-inch pie pan. Trim edge and prick bottom and side with a fork. Slice the strawberries lengthwise. Combine the sugar and cornstarch, then layer the strawberries and sugar mixture in the pie shell. Roll out the remaining dough and cut into strips with a pastry wheel. Arrange strips over top of pie in lattice fashion. Press strip around edge, sealing together. Brush with the egg. Bake at 400 degrees for 30 to 35 minutes or until pastry is brown. Cool before serving.

Photograph for this recipe on page 12.

GREEN TOMATO PIE

1 2/3 c. sugar	3 tbsp. grated lemon rind
3 tbsp. flour	1/4 tsp. salt
3 1/2 c. thinly sliced green	1/4 c. butter
tomatoes	Pastry for 2-crust pie
3 tbsp. lemon juice	

Combine the sugar and flour in a bowl and stir in remaining ingredients except butter and pastry. Place in pastry-lined pie pan and dot with butter. Add the top crust and cut slits in center. Bake at 450 degrees for 10 minutes. Reduce temperature to 350 degrees and bake for 30 minutes longer. Serve with wedges of cheese, if desired.

Mrs. R. D. Smallwood, Worthington, West Virginia

WATERMELON PIE

Watermelon rind	Pinch of salt
1 c. sugar	2 tbsp. flour
1 tsp. cinnamon	1/4 c. vinegar
1/3 tsp. nutmeg	1/2 c. raisins (opt.)
1/4 tsp. cloves	Pastry for 2-crust pie

Cut the green rind and most of the pink from watermelon rind. Cut enough of the rind into 1/4-inch cubes to make 1 1/2 cups rind. Place in a saucepan and cover with water. Cook until tender, then drain. Add remaining ingredients except pastry. Place in a pastry-lined pie pan and cover with top crust. Cut slits in center. Bake at 450 degrees for 10 minutes. Reduce temperature to 350 degrees and bake for about 30 minutes or until done.

Mrs. Jim West, Newark, Delaware

cream pies

Smoothly elegant and utterly delicious, cream pies are favorite desserts at ladies' luncheons . . . afternoon gatherings . . . dinners . . . or for late evening snacks. They come in as many flavors as your imagination can create — and this variety makes them even more of a homemaker's favorite!

Cream pies are certainly favored desserts with the ladies of the Southland, as the recipes that follow illustrate. Turning these pages, you'll find cream pie recipes using chocolate . . . fruit . . . nuts . . . even ice cream. Every recipe is the home-tested, family-approved favorite of the homemaker who now shares it with you. They're all certain to be favorites with your family, too.

Just imagine how delighted everyone around your dinner table will be when you carry in an elegant Key Lime Pie. This typically southern pie got its start at one of the great Florida hotels — the prized recipe is shared with you in this section. There are other marvelous recipes, too, like Chocolate Chip-Almond Pie . . . Peach Parfait Pie . . . Angel Food Strawberry Pie . . . and many more.

Treat your family to one of these easy-to-prepare pies soon. They're perfect for those days when you don't want to do a lot of baking. Just prepare a pie shell — perhaps one of the no-bake crumb shells. Mix the filling you choose, pour it into the shell, and chill. That's all the work it takes to bring compliments your way!

BEAUTIFUL MERINGUE FOR PIE

1/2 c. water	3 egg whites
1 tbsp. cornstarch	1/4 tsp. cream of tartar
1/2 c. sugar	

Combine the water, cornstarch and 2 tablespoons sugar in a saucepan and mix well. Cook until thick, stirring constantly, then cool. Beat egg whites with cream of tartar in a bowl until stiff. Add remaining sugar gradually and beat until glossy. Fold in cornstarch mixture and spread on pie. Bake at 350 degrees until brown.

Mrs. M. M. Erion, Little Rock, Arkansas

NEVER-FAIL MERINGUE

3 egg whites	6 tbsp. sugar
1/4 tsp. cream of tartar	1/2 tsp. vanilla

Beat the egg whites and cream of tartar in a bowl until fluffy. Add the sugar gradually and beat until stiff peaks form. Add the vanilla and beat well. Spread on pie so that meringue touches edge of crust. Bake in 400-degree oven for 8 to 10 minutes or until brown.

Mary Carter, Lexington, Kentucky

APPLESAUCE PIE

1 1/2 c. graham cracker crumbs	1/4 c. chopped pecans
1/2 c. melted butter	Dash of cinnamon
5/8 c. sugar	2 egg whites
1/2 c. crushed pineapple	1 tsp. pineapple juice
2 1/3 c. applesauce	

Blend the crumbs, butter and 2 tablespoons sugar in a bowl, then press into pie plate. Chill until firm. Mix the applesauce, 1/4 cup sugar and pineapple and place in the pie crust. Sprinkle with pecans and cinnamon. Beat the egg whites in a bowl until stiff, adding remaining sugar and pineapple juice gradually. Spread on pie. Bake at 400 degrees for 10 minutes or until brown. Cool.

Mrs. Henry Lamar, Knoxville, Tennessee

BANANA-CARAMEL PIE

1 can sweetened condensed milk	Sweetened whipped cream
3 bananas, sliced	1/2 c. chopped pecans
1 8-in. vanilla wafer crust	

Place the unopened can of sweetened condensed milk in a saucepan and cover with water. Bring to a boil and reduce heat. Simmer for 3 hours, adding water as needed to keep can covered. Cool. Place half the bananas in the pie crust and add half the caramelized milk. Add remaining bananas and top with remaining caramelized milk. Cover with whipped cream and sprinkle pecans over whipped cream.

Mrs. Travis Dixson, Irving, Texas

BANANA CREAM PIE

3/4 c. sugar	2 tbsp. margarine
1/4 c. flour	1 tsp. vanilla
1/4 tsp. salt	2 bananas, sliced
2 c. milk	1 baked 9-in. pastry shell
2 eggs, separated	

Mix 1/2 cup sugar, flour and salt in top of a double boiler and stir in small amount of the milk. Stir in remaining milk and cook over boiling water, stirring, until thick. Cover and cook for 15 minutes longer, stirring occasionally. Add small amount of the hot mixture to beaten egg yolks. Stir back into hot mixture and cook for several minutes longer. Add margarine and vanilla and stir until margarine is melted. Place the bananas in the pie shell and pour filling over bananas. Cool slightly. Beat the egg whites in a bowl until stiff, adding remaining sugar gradually. Spread over filling. Bake at 400 degrees for 10 minutes or until light brown.

Mrs. Ina Moore, Ringgold, Louisiana

BANANA ICEBOX PIE

1 can sweetened condensed milk	1 baked 9-in. pastry shell
1/4 c. lemon juice	Whipped cream
2 lge. bananas, sliced	

Blend the milk and lemon juice in a bowl, then fold in bananas. Pour into the pastry shell. Chill. Cover with whipped cream just before serving.

Mrs. Hettie Patton, Manila, Arkansas

QUICK BANANA-COCONUT PIE

1/4 c. melted butter	2 c. milk
2 c. flaked coconut	2 bananas, sliced
1 pkg. vanilla pudding mix	Sweetened whipped cream

Mix the butter and coconut and press into bottom and side of a 9-inch pie pan. Bake at 350 degrees for about 3 minutes or until golden brown. Cool. Combine the pie filling and milk in a saucepan. Cook, stirring, over medium heat until mixture comes to a boil. Remove from heat and cool for 5 minutes, stirring occasionally. Pour half the mixture into the coconut crust. Cover with bananas and add remaining filling. Chill. Spread a circle of whipped cream around edge of pie and just before serving sprinkle with additional flaked coconut.

Mrs. Macie Fountain, McIntyre, Georgia

BUTTERSCOTCH BANANA PIE

2 c. milk
2/3 c. (packed) light
   brown sugar
1/3 c. flour
3/4 tsp. salt

3 eggs, slightly beaten
2 tsp. butter
1 tsp. vanilla
1 baked 9-in. pie shell
3 ripe bananas, sliced

Scald the milk in a heavy saucepan. Combine the brown sugar, flour and salt, then stir into the milk slowly. Cook, stirring constantly, for about 10 minutes or until thick. Stir a small amount of the hot mixture into the eggs, then stir into remaining hot mixture. Cook for 1 minute longer. Remove from heat and stir in the butter and vanilla, then cool thoroughly. Cover the bottom of the pie shell with a small amount of filling, then add alternate layers of sliced bananas and butterscotch filling, ending with filling. Chill thoroughly. Garnish with additional banana slices. Top with sweetened whipped cream, if desired.

BLACKBERRY CREAM PIE

1 can sweetened condensed milk
1/4 c. lemon juice
2 c. fresh blackberries

1 baked pie shell
1/2 pt. whipping cream
1/4 c. sugar

Combine the milk and lemon juice in a bowl and mix well. Stir in blackberries and place in the pie shell. Chill. Whip the cream in a bowl until stiff, adding sugar gradually. Spread on the pie just before serving.

Mrs. Aaron Owens, Winchester, Tennessee

BLUEBERRY-CREAM PIE

1 3-oz. package cream cheese	1 baked 9-in. pie shell
1 c. powdered sugar	1 can blueberry pie filling
2 c. sweetened whipped cream	

Beat the cream cheese and powdered sugar in a bowl with mixer until smooth and fold in whipped cream. Pour into the pie shell and refrigerate for about 2 hours or until firm. Spoon pie filling onto cream mixture. May be topped with additional whipped cream, if desired.

Mrs. Robert A. Sell, Winston-Salem, North Carolina

BUTTERMILK PIE

1/2 c. softened butter	1 c. buttermilk
2 c. sugar	1 tsp. vanilla
3 tbsp. flour	1 unbaked 9-in. pie shell
3 eggs, beaten	

Cream the butter and sugar in a bowl. Add the flour and eggs and beat well. Stir in the buttermilk and vanilla and pour into pie shell. Bake at 350 degrees for 45 to 50 minutes. Cool thoroughly.

Roberta Capps, Fayetteville, North Carolina

BUTTERSCOTCH PIE

2 c. flour	2/3 c. shortening
1/2 tsp. salt	Ice water

Sift the flour and salt together into a bowl and cut in shortening. Add just enough ice water to hold ingredients together. Divide pastry in half and roll out each half between 2 sheets of waxed paper. Fit into 2 pie pans and prick pastry with tines of fork. Bake at 425 degrees until brown.

Filling

2 c. (firmly packed) light brown sugar	1 c. cold water
3 tbsp. (heaping) flour	3 eggs, separated
1/2 tsp. salt	1 tsp. vanilla
2 tbsp. hot water	3 tbsp. butter
1 c. milk	6 tbsp. sugar

Mix the brown sugar, flour and salt in top of a double boiler and stir in hot water slowly. Add the milk, cold water and beaten egg yolks and mix well. Cook over boiling water until thick, stirring constantly. Remove from water and beat in vanilla and butter. Pour into pie shells. Beat the egg whites in a bowl until soft peaks form, then beat until stiff, adding sugar gradually. Spread on pies. Bake at 425 degrees until brown.

Mrs. Vernon Cundiff, Ravenna, Kentucky

CARAMEL PIE

1 c. flour	1/3 c. shortening
1/2 tsp. salt	3 tsp. cold water

Mix the flour and salt in a bowl and cut in the shortening. Add the water and mix. Roll out on a floured surface 1 inch larger than pie pan and place in the pan. Turn pastry under and flute edge. Prick pastry with tines of fork. Bake at 450 degrees for 8 to 10 minutes or until brown.

Filling

1 3/8 c. sugar	Pinch of salt
3 tbsp. flour	1 tsp. vanilla
3 eggs, separated	1 tsp. ice water
1 1/4 c. milk	Pinch of cream of tartar

Mix 1/2 cup sugar with the flour. Beat the egg yolks well in top of a double boiler. Stir in the flour mixture, then the milk. Cook over boiling water until thick, stirring frequently. Place 1/2 cup sugar in a heavy skillet and cook over low heat, stirring constantly, until sugar is melted and golden brown. Add to egg mixture slowly, stirring constantly. Add the salt and vanilla and pour into pie shell. Beat the egg whites with ice water and cream of tartar in a bowl until stiff, adding sugar gradually. Spread on pie. Bake at 400 degrees until brown.

Mrs. C. D. Goodwin, Columbus, Mississippi

CHERRY CREAM PIE

6 tbsp. flour	3 egg yolks, beaten
6 tbsp. sugar	1 tsp. vanilla
1/8 tsp. salt	1 baked 9-in. pie shell
2 c. milk	

Mix the flour, sugar and salt in a saucepan. Stir in the milk and egg yolks and mix well. Cook over medium heat until thick, stirring constantly. Remove from heat and add vanilla. Cool. Pour into pie shell.

Cherry Topping

1 No. 303 can cherries	1/8 tsp. salt
2 tbsp. flour	Whipped cream
1/2 c. sugar	

Drain the cherries and reserve juice. Add enough water to reserved juice to make 1 cup liquid. Combine the flour, sugar and salt in a saucepan and add the cherry liquid slowly, stirring constantly. Cook over medium heat, stirring, until thickened. Add the cherries and cool. Place on the cream mixture in pie shell and cover with whipped cream. Refrigerate until chilled.

Mrs. Karen Calico, Huntsville, Arkansas

SPICY CHERRY MERINGUE PIE

3/4 c. sugar	1 baked 8-in. pastry shell
2 tbsp. cornstarch	2 egg whites
1 17-oz. can water-pack	1/4 tsp. almond flavoring
cherries	2 tbsp. cinnamon sugar

Combine 1/2 cup sugar and cornstarch in a saucepan. Drain the juice from cherries, then stir the juice into the sugar mixture. Add the cherries and bring to a boil. Boil 1 minute, stirring constantly. Pour into the pastry shell. Beat the egg whites until foamy, then add the remaining sugar, 1 tablespoon at a time, beating well after each addition. Continue beating until stiff peaks form when beater is raised. Beat in the flavoring. Spread meringue around edge of shell to touch all around and seal, then fill in center. Sprinkle with cinnamon sugar. Bake at 350 degrees for 15 to 20 minutes or until meringue is lightly browned. Cool at room temperature, away from drafts.

HEAVENLY HASH PIE

1 1/2 c. graham cracker crumbs	1 can sour pitted cherries
1/2 c. melted butter or	1 can sweetened condensed milk
margarine	1/2 c. lemon juice
2 tbsp. sugar	1 c. chopped pecans

Mix the crumbs, butter and sugar and reserve 1/2 cup. Press remaining crumb mixture on bottom and side of a 9-inch pie pan and chill for 2 hours. Drain the cherries well. Add remaining ingredients and stir until mixed. Pour into crust and sprinkle with reserved crumbs. Chill.

Mrs. George Willis, Girard, Georgia

CHOCOLATE CHARM PIE

1 c. milk	2 sq. unsweetened chocolate,
1/2 lb. marshmallows	melted
1/8 tsp. salt	1/2 c. chopped nuts
1 tsp. vanilla	1 baked 9-in. pie shell
1 pkg. dessert topping mix	1/4 c. flaked coconut

Heat the milk in a saucepan. Add the marshmallows and stir until melted. Chill until thickened. Stir in the salt and vanilla. Prepare the dessert topping mix according to package directions and add to marshmallow mixture. Stir in the chocolate and nuts and pour into pie shell. Sprinkle with coconut. Chill until firm.

Mrs. Harvey Allen, Bluefield, West Virginia

CHOCOLATE CHIP-ALMOND PIE

6 sm. chocolate-almond bars	1/2 c. chocolate chips
17 marshmallows	1/2 c. slivered almonds
1/2 c. milk	1 baked graham cracker crust
1 c. whipping cream, whipped	

Place the chocolate bars, marshmallows and milk in top of a double boiler and cook over boiling water until melted, stirring frequently. Cool. Fold in whipped cream, chocolate chips and almonds and pour into graham cracker crust. Garnish with additional chocolate chips. Refrigerate for at least 4 hours.

Mrs. J. C. Fryday, La Porte, Texas

CHOCOLATE ICE BOX PIE

1/2 c. softened butter	2 sq. unsweetened chocolate
3/4 c. sugar	1 baked pie shell
1 tsp. vanilla	Whipped cream
2 eggs	

Place the butter, sugar and vanilla in a bowl and beat with an electric mixer until blended. Add the eggs, one at a time, beating for 5 minutes after each addition. Melt the chocolate over hot water and blend into the egg mixture. Pour into the pie shell and chill for at least 2 hours. Serve with whipped cream.

Mrs. William W. Bradford, Columbus, Mississippi

FRIENDSHIP HOUSE CHOCOLATE PIE

1 1/2 c. sugar	1/4 tsp. salt
1/2 c. cornstarch	2 1/2 c. milk
1/2 c. cocoa	3 egg yolks, beaten

1/2 tsp. vanilla
1   9-in. baked pie shell

1/2 pt. whipping cream,
    whipped

Mix the sugar, cornstarch, cocoa and salt in top of a double boiler. Add 1/2 cup milk and egg yolks and blend well. Add remaining milk. Place over boiling water and cook, stirring, until thick. Add vanilla. Pour into the pie shell and top with whipped cream. Chill.

Mrs. B. B. Nelson, Eau Gallie, Florida

DELUXE CHOCOLATE CREAM PIE

1 env. unflavored gelatin
1/4 c. cold water
1 c. fortified chocolate-
    flavored syrup

1 pt. heavy cream, whipped
1/2 tsp. rum or almond extract
1 baked 9-in. pastry shell

Sprinkle the gelatin over the water and soften for 5 minutes. Place the chocolate syrup in a medium-sized saucepan and bring to a boil. Remove from heat and stir in the gelatin until dissolved. Chill, stirring occasionally, until thick and syrupy. Fold the whipped cream into the chocolate mixture, then fold in the rum extract. Pile into the pastry shell. Chill until firm.

COCONUT-BUTTERSCOTCH PIE

3/4 c. sifted flour	1/4 c. butter
1 1/2 c. (packed) brown sugar	1 1/2 tsp. vanilla
1/4 tsp. salt	1 1/2 c. flaked coconut
3 c. scalded milk	1 baked 9-in. pie shell
3 eggs, separated	6 tbsp. sugar

Combine the flour, brown sugar and salt in top of a double boiler and stir in milk gradually. Cook over boiling water until thickened, stirring constantly. Stir small amount of milk mixture into egg yolks. Stir back into milk mixture and cook for 3 to 4 minutes longer, stirring frequently. Remove from heat and add butter, vanilla and 1 cup coconut. Cool, then pour into pie shell. Beat the egg whites in a bowl until stiff, adding sugar gradually, and spread over coconut mixture. Sprinkle with remaining coconut. Bake at 350 degrees for 12 to 15 minutes or until light brown.

Mrs. Ray Kirby, Gaffney, South Carolina

COCONUT ICE CREAM PIE

2 tbsp. flour	1 c. shredded coconut
1/4 tsp. salt	1 tbsp. butter
2 tbsp. cornstarch	2 egg whites, well beaten
2 c. milk	1 baked pie crust
3/4 c. sugar	

Mix the flour, salt and cornstarch in top of a double boiler. Stir in the milk slowly. Add the sugar and stir until sugar is dissolved. Cook over boiling water until thickened, stirring frequently. Add 1/2 cup coconut and stir. Add the butter and stir until butter is melted. Fold in the egg whites. Pour into the crust and sprinkle with remaining coconut. Chill.

Mrs. Richard R. Holter, Jefferson, Maryland

EGGNOG PIE

1 tsp. unflavored gelatin	3 egg yolks, beaten
1 tbsp. cold water	1 1/2 tsp. vanilla
1/2 c. sugar	1/4 tsp. almond extract
2 tbsp. cornstarch	1 c. whipping cream, whipped
1/4 tsp. salt	1 9-in. baked pie shell
1 c. milk, scalded	Nutmeg

Soften the gelatin in cold water in a small bowl. Mix the sugar, cornstarch and salt in a double boiler. Stir in the milk slowly and cook until thick, stirring frequently. Stir small amount of milk mixture into egg yolks. Stir back into milk mixture and cook for several minutes longer. Remove from heat. Add the gelatin, vanilla and almond extract and cool, stirring occasionally to prevent skim forming on top. Fold in the whipped cream. Pour into pie shell and sprinkle heavily with nutmeg. Chill overnight.

Florence Harris, Meridian, Mississippi

FRENCH MINT PIE

1/3 c. butter or margarine	1 1/4 c. chocolate wafer crumbs

Mix the butter and wafer crumbs and press firmly on bottom and side of an 8-inch pie pan. Bake at 350 degrees for 10 minutes. Cool.

Filling

1/2 c. butter or margarine	2 eggs, well beaten
1 1/2 c. sifted confectioners' sugar	1/2 tsp. vanilla
2 sq. bitter chocolate, melted	4 drops of oil of peppermint

Cream the butter and sugar in a bowl. Add the chocolate and mix well. Add the eggs, vanilla and oil of peppermint and beat until light. Pour into the crust and chill overnight.

Ona Ragsdale, Mountain Home, Arkansas

GELATIN-MANGO PIE

1 pkg. peach gelatin	Pinch of salt
1 1/4 c. hot water	1 1/2 c. thinly sliced mangos
1 pt. vanilla ice cream	1 baked 8-in. pastry shell

Dissolve the gelatin in hot water in a bowl. Add ice cream and salt and stir until melted. Chill in freezer for 15 to 20 minutes or until syrupy. Fold in mangos and pour into pastry shell. Chill for 1 hour or until firm. Garnish with additional sliced mangos.

S. A. Love, Miami, Florida

BLACK BOTTOM LEMON PIE

2 1-oz. squares semisweet chocolate	1/4 c. lemon juice
1 baked 9-in. pie shell	3 tbsp. water
4 eggs, separated	1 tsp. grated lemon peel
	1 c. sugar

Melt the chocolate over hot water and spread over the pie shell. Beat the egg yolks in top of a double boiler until thick and lemon-colored. Add the lemon juice and water and mix well. Stir in the lemon peel and 1/2 cup sugar and cook over hot, not boiling, water for about 12 minutes or until thick, stirring constantly. Remove from heat. Beat the egg whites in a bowl until frothy. Add remaining sugar gradually and beat until stiff peaks form. Fold half the meringue into egg yolk mixture and spread over chocolate. Spoon remaining meringue into a pastry tube and pipe onto egg yolk mixture in lattice design. Bake at 325 degrees for 10 to 15 minutes or until meringue is lightly browned. Cool.

Mrs. J. A. Hanna, Pascagoula, Mississippi

LEMON-COCONUT GLAMOR PIE

1/2 c. butter	2 tsp. grated lemon peel
1 1/4 c. sugar	1 baked 9-in. pie shell
4 eggs	1/2 c. flaked coconut
6 tbsp. lemon juice	

Combine the butter and 1 cup sugar in top of a double boiler. Add 2 eggs, 2 egg yolks, lemon juice and grated peel and beat well. Cook over boiling water, stirring constantly, until thick, then chill. Pour into pie shell. Beat the egg whites in a bowl until stiff, adding remaining sugar gradually. Spread on lemon mixture and sprinkle with coconut. Bake at 400 degrees for 8 to 10 minutes or until golden brown.

Mrs. R. A. Pippenger, Bradford, Arkansas

FRESH LEMON MERINGUE PIE

3 to 4 California lemons	2 tbsp. butter or
Sugar	margarine
6 tbsp. cornstarch	1 1/2 c. boiling water
1/4 tsp. salt	1/4 tsp. cream of tartar
1/2 c. cold water	1 baked 9-in. pie shell
3 eggs, separated	

Grate 1 teaspoon peel from lemon and squeeze out 1/2 cup juice. Set aside. Combine 1 1/2 cups sugar, cornstarch and salt in a saucepan thoroughly and blend in lemon juice, cold water and beaten egg yolks until completely smooth. Add the butter and stir in the boiling water gradually. Bring to a boil and cook for 3 to 4 minutes, stirring constantly. Stir in the grated peel and cool. Beat the egg whites just until frothy, then add the cream of tartar and beat at high speed until soft peaks form. Add 6 tablespoons sugar gradually, beating until all sugar is used and whites are stiff, but not dry. Pour filling into baked pie shell. Spread the meringue over filling, sealing carefully at edges of pastry. Bake at 350 degrees for 12 to 15 minutes or until golden brown. Cool on rack away from drafts.

Photograph for this recipe on cover.

MAGIC LEMON MERINGUE PIE

1 c. fine graham cracker crumbs	1/2 c. lemon juice
3 tbsp. softened margarine	1 tbsp. grated lemon peel
1 can sweetened condensed milk	1/4 tsp. cream of tartar
2 eggs, separated	1/4 c. sugar

Blend the crumbs with margarine and press firmly into an 8-inch pie plate. Mix the milk and egg yolks in a bowl. Add the lemon juice and grated peel and stir until well blended. Pour into crust. Beat the egg whites with cream of tartar in a bowl until foamy. Add the sugar gradually and beat until stiff but not dry. Spread over filling, sealing to crust. Bake at 325 degrees for about 15 minutes or until brown. Cool.

Evelyn Marie Frasier, Wadmalaw Island, South Carolina

FOOLPROOF LEMON CHEESE PIE

2 slices bread, crusts removed
1 3/8 c. sugar
3 eggs, separated
1/4 c. butter or margarine

Juice and grated rind of 2
   lemons
Pinch of salt
1 baked pie shell

Soak the bread in just enough water to cover, then squeeze out most of the water. Mix 1 cup sugar, egg yolks, bread, butter, lemon juice, grated rind and salt in a saucepan and cook, stirring constantly, until thick. Place in the pie shell. Beat the egg whites in a bowl until stiff, adding remaining sugar gradually. Spread over lemon mixture. Bake at 400 degrees until lightly browned.

Mrs. Joe Flournoy, Columbus, Georgia

LEMON CREAM PIE

1/4 c. cornstarch
5 tbsp. flour
1 1/2 c. sugar
2 c. boiling water
2 tbsp. butter

4 egg yolks, beaten
Grated rind of 2 lemons
6 tbsp. lemon juice
1 baked 9-in. pastry shell
1 recipe meringue

Mix the cornstarch, flour and sugar in a saucepan, then add boiling water gradually, stirring constantly. Cook over low heat for 10 minutes, stirring constantly. Add butter, egg yolks, grated rind and lemon juice and blend thoroughly. Cook until thick, stirring constantly, and pour into pie shell. Cover with meringue. Bake at 325 degrees for 10 to 15 minutes or until lightly browned.

Mrs. Beulah S. Campbell, Taylors, South Carolina

GRAPEFRUIT PIE

1 pkg. pink grapefruit gelatin
1 c. boiling water
1 pt. grapefruit or lime
   sherbet

1 No. 2 can sweetened
   grapefruit sections, drained
1 baked pie shell
Dessert topping

Dissolve the gelatin in boiling water in a bowl and stir in the sherbet until dissolved. Cut the grapefruit sections in small pieces and stir into gelatin mixture. Spoon into pie shell and chill until firm. Cover with dessert topping just before serving.

Fannie R. Weale, Leesburg, Florida

KEY LIME CHEESE PIE

1 1/4 c. graham cracker crumbs
Sugar
1/3 c. margarine, melted
1 c. creamed cottage cheese

1 pkg. Key Lime pie filling
2 c. cold water
2 eggs, separated

Combine the crumbs and 3 tablespoons sugar in a bowl, then blend in the margarine. Press the mixture firmly and evenly against bottom and side of a 9-inch pie pan. Bake at 350 degrees for about 8 to 10 minutes. Cool thoroughly before filling. Press the cottage cheese through a sieve or whip cheese thoroughly until smooth. Combine the pie filling and 1/2 cup sugar in saucepan, then add the cold water and slightly beaten egg yolks gradually, stirring to keep mixture smooth. Cook over medium high heat, stirring constantly, until mixture begins to boil and flavor capsule is dissolved. Stir the hot filling into the cottage cheese until thoroughly blended. Cool for about 10 minutes. Beat the egg whites until foamy, then add 1/4 cup sugar gradually, beating until glossy and stiff. Stir the hot lime filling, then fold the filling into the meringue gradually. Turn into the pie crust. Chill for at least 4 hours or until set.

KEY LIME PIE

1 can sweetened condensed milk
1/2 c. lime juice

Grated rind of 1 lime
2 eggs, separated

1 graham cracker crust   1/4 c. sugar
1/4 tsp. cream of tartar

Blend the milk with lime juice, grated rind and egg yolks in a bowl. Pour into the graham cracker crust. Beat the egg whites and cream of tartar in a bowl until foamy. Add the sugar gradually and beat until stiff peaks form. Spread over filling, sealing to edge of crust. Bake at 425 degrees for about 4 minutes or until brown.

Mrs. George McCarty, Fort Myers Beach, Florida

LIME-PINEAPPLE PARFAIT PIE

1 No. 2 can crushed pineapple   1 baked 9-in. pie shell
1 3-oz. package lime gelatin   Fresh lime slices
1 pt. vanilla ice cream

Drain the pineapple and reserve juice. Add enough water to reserved juice to make 1 1/4 cups liquid and pour into a saucepan. Bring to a boil and remove from heat. Add the gelatin and stir until dissolved. Add the ice cream by spoonfuls and stir until melted. Chill until thickened. Fold in the pineapple and turn into the pie shell. Chill until firm. Garnish with twisted fresh lime slices.

Mrs. R. V. Olsen, St. Stephen, South Carolina

LIME-TAMER PIE

1 1/2 c. flaked coconut   1 3 1/2-oz. package lime pie filling
2 tbsp. soft butter   1 c. thinly sliced bananas
1 unbaked 9-in. pie shell   1 recipe meringue

Mix 1 cup coconut and the butter and spread over bottom and side of pie shell. Bake at 475 degrees for 8 to 10 minutes. Cool. Prepare pie filling according to package directions and cool slightly. Fold in the bananas and pour into pie shell. Top with meringue and sprinkle with remaining coconut. Bake at 425 degrees for about 5 minutes. Cool thoroughly.

Mrs. J. A. Senter, Lillington, North Carolina

MUSCATEL PIE

22 lge. marshmallows   1 9-in. graham cracker crust
1/3 c. muscatel   Sliced toasted almonds to taste
1/2 pt. whipped cream

Place the marshmallows and wine in top of a double boiler. Cook over boiling water until marshmallows are melted, stirring frequently. Cool, then fold in the whipped cream. Place in the pie crust and refrigerate until chilled. Sprinkle with almonds just before serving.

Martha Smith, North Little Rock, Arkansas

WHIPPED ORANGE VELVET PIE

1 3-oz. package orange gelatin	1 c. evaporated milk
1/2 c. sugar	2 tbsp. lemon juice
2/3 c. hot water	1 9-in. chocolate crumb crust
1/2 c. hot orange juice	

Dissolve the gelatin and sugar in the hot water and orange juice. Chill until the consistency of unbeaten egg white. Chill the evaporated milk in a refrigerator tray for 15 to 20 minutes or until soft ice crystals form around edges of tray. Whip for 1 minute or until stiff, then add the lemon juice and whip for about 2 minutes longer. Fold into the chilled gelatin mixture. Spoon into the crumb crust and chill for about 2 hours or until firm. Garnish with orange wedges, if desired.

Crumb Crust

1 1/2 c. chocolate cookie crumbs	2 tbsp. sugar
	1/4 c. melted butter

Mix the crumbs, sugar and butter together, then line the side and bottom of 9-inch pie plate with the crumb mixture.

CREAMY MANDARIN ORANGE PIE

1 4-oz. can mandarin oranges	3/4 c. milk
1 baked 9-in. pie shell	1/2 pt. whipping cream
2 or 3 firm bananas	1/2 tsp. vanilla
1 pkg. instant banana pudding mix	1 sm. can flaked coconut

Drain the oranges and arrange in pie shell. Slice the bananas over orange slices. Combine pudding mix, milk, whipping cream and vanilla and beat with mixer until slightly thickened. Pour over sliced fruit and sprinkle with coconut. Refrigerate for 1 hour or longer before serving.

Mrs. Justus J. Bird, South Charleston, West Virginia

ORANGE JUICE PIE

1 c. sugar	1 tbsp. butter
1/4 tsp. salt	3 tbsp. lemon juice
1/3 c. flour	2 tbsp. grated orange rind
1 c. orange juice	1 baked 9-in. pie shell
2 eggs, separated	5 tbsp. confectioners' sugar

Combine sugar, salt and flour in top of double boiler, then stir in the orange juice. Cook, stirring constantly, for about 5 minutes or until thickened. Cover and let steam for 15 minutes. Beat the egg yolks and stir a small amount of juice mixture into egg yolks. Add butter to juice mixture, then stir in egg yolk mixture. Cook for 2 to 3 minutes longer, stirring constantly, then remove from heat. Add lemon juice and orange rind. Cool and pour into pie shell. Beat the egg whites until soft peaks form, then add confectioners' sugar gradually, beating until stiff peaks form. Spread over filling. Bake at 350 degrees for 15 minutes or until browned.

Mildred Wise Howe, Dillwyn, Virginia

PEACH PARFAIT PIE

3 1/2 c. sweetened peaches	1 9-in. baked pie shell
1 pkg. lemon gelatin	1/2 c. heavy cream, whipped
1 pt. vanilla ice cream	

Drain the peaches, reserving syrup, then add water to reserved syrup to make 1 cup liquid. Bring to a boil and add the gelatin. Stir until dissolved. Add 1/2 cup cold water. Cut the ice cream into 6 pieces, then add to the gelatin mixture and stir until melted. Chill for 15 to 20 minutes or until mounds form slightly when dropped from a spoon. Fold in the peach slices and pour into pie shell. Chill until firm. Garnish with whipped cream and additional peaches.

Mrs. Lila Quincy, Arlington, Virginia

PEANUT BUTTER PIE

1 c. graham cracker crumbs	1 pkg. vanilla pudding mix
1/4 c. melted butter	1 1/2 o. milk
1/4 c. sugar	1/4 c. peanut butter

Mix the crumbs, melted butter and sugar, then pat into a 9-inch pie pan. Bake at 350 degrees for 8 minutes. Prepare pudding mix according to package directions using milk. Stir in the peanut butter. Cool and pour into crust. Garnish with whipped cream to serve.

Mrs. Frank Underwood, Choctaw, Oklahoma

PEANUT CREAM PIE

1 c. milk	1 tbsp. butter
Sugar	1/2 c. ground parched peanuts
3 tbsp. flour	1 baked pie shell
1 egg, separated	

Pour the milk in a saucepan. Sift 2/3 cup sugar and flour together, then stir into the milk. Bring to a boil. Add small amount of milk mixture to beaten egg yolk, then stir back into milk mixture and add the butter. Cook until thick and smooth, stirring constantly. Stir in the peanuts and pour into pie shell. Beat the egg white until soft peaks form, then add 1 tablespoon sugar and beat until stiff peaks form. Spread over the pie. Bake at 350 degrees until browned.

Lula B. Jones, San Angelo, Texas

PECAN CREAM PIE

1 c. sugar	1/2 c. finely ground pecans
3 tbsp. flour	1 tsp. vanilla
1 1/2 c. evaporated milk	1 baked pie shell
2 egg yolks, beaten	1 recipe meringue

Combine the sugar, flour, milk and egg yolks in a saucepan and mix well. Cook until thickened, stirring constantly. Add the pecans and vanilla, then pour into the pie shell. Spread the meringue over the top. Bake at 350 degrees until browned.

Mrs. W. A. Shores, Abbeville, Louisiana

PINEAPPLE-RICE PIE

1 can sweetened condensed milk	1 c. cooked rice
1/2 c. lemon juice	1/2 c. drained crushed
Grated rind of 1 lemon	pineapple
2 egg yolks	1 baked pie shell
2 tbsp. sugar	1 recipe meringue

Blend the milk, lemon juice, lemon rind, egg yolks and sugar together, then fold in the rice and pineapple. Pour into pie shell. Chill for about 2 hours. Cover with meringue. Bake at 350 degrees for 10 minutes or until browned.

Mrs. Norman Prose, Weiner, Arkansas

PINEAPPLE MERINGUE PIE

1 1-lb. 4 1/2-oz. can crushed	3/4 c. sugar
pineapple	2 tbsp. flour

1/8 tsp. salt
1 c. sour cream
3 egg yolks, beaten

1 tbsp. lemon juice
1 baked pie shell

Drain the pineapple and reserve 1/2 cup syrup. Combine the sugar, flour and salt in a medium saucepan, then stir in the pineapple, reserved syrup, sour cream, egg yolks and lemon juice. Cook over medium heat, stirring constantly, until thick. Cover and cool to lukewarm, then pour into pie shell.

Never-Fail Meringue

8 tbsp. sugar
1 tbsp. cornstarch
3 egg whites

1/8 tsp. salt
1/2 tsp. vanilla

Combine 2 tablespoons sugar with the cornstarch in a small saucepan and add 1/2 cup water. Cook over medium heat, stirring constantly, until mixture is thick and clear. Beat the egg whites with the salt and vanilla until soft peaks form. Add the remaining sugar gradually, beating well after each addition. Add the hot mixture slowly, beating until meringue stands in stiff peaks. Spoon over filling. Bake at 350 degrees for 12 to 15 minutes or until golden brown.

Mrs. Temple Busley, Kaufman, Texas

PINEAPPLE PARFAIT PIE

1 No. 2 can crushed pineapple
1 sm. package lemon gelatin

1 pt. vanilla ice cream
1 baked pie shell, cooled

Drain the pineapple and reserve syrup. Add enough water to reserved syrup to make 3/4 cup liquid and pour into a saucepan. Bring to a boil and remove from heat. Add the gelatin and stir until dissolved. Add the ice cream and stir until melted. Chill until thickened and fold in pineapple. Turn into pie shell and chill until firm. Top with whipped cream, if desired.

Mrs. A. L. Hallman, Charlotte, North Carolina

PINEAPPLE-CHERRY-BANANA PIE

1 No. 303 can sour red
   cherries
1 No. 2 can crushed pineapple
2 c. sugar
1/4 c. cornstarch
1 tsp. vanilla

1 tsp. red food coloring
1 c. chopped pecans
6 sliced bananas
2 baked 9-in. pie shells
2 c. whipped cream

Drain the cherries and pineapple and add enough water to the juice to make 2 cups liquid. Mix the sugar and cornstarch and stir into the juice mixture. Cook, stirring, until thick. Add vanilla and food coloring, then cool thoroughly. Add the drained fruits and pecans. Alternate layers of the cherry mixture and sliced bananas in the pie shells. Top with whipped cream to serve.

Mrs. Lillian Herman, Bay City, Texas

PUMPKIN MERINGUE PIE

3/4 c. sugar	3 egg yolks, beaten
1/3 c. flour	1 c. cooked mashed pumpkin
1/2 tsp. salt	1 c. coconut
1/2 tsp. baking powder	1 tsp. vanilla
1 1/2 c. milk	1 baked pie shell

Blend the sugar, flour, salt and baking powder together, then stir in the milk gradually. Add the egg yolks and pumpkin and mix well. Cook for about 20 minutes or until creamy, stirring frequently. Remove from the heat and stir in the coconut and vanilla. Pour in the pie shell.

Meringue

3 egg whites	1 tsp. vanilla
Dash of salt	1/4 c. coconut
1/3 c. sugar	

Beat the egg whites with the salt until soft peaks form, then add the sugar and vanilla gradually, beating until stiff peaks form. Spread the meringue over the pie, sealing to crust. Sprinkle with coconut. Bake at 350 degrees until browned. Cool before serving.

Mrs. L. W. Jernigan, Wauchula, Florida

PUMPKIN-WHIPPED CREAM PIE

1 1/2 c. graham cracker crumbs	1/2 c. melted butter
1 tbsp. sugar	1/2 c. chopped pecans
1/8 tsp. cinnamon	

Combine the graham cracker crumbs, sugar, cinnamon and butter in a bowl and mix well. Press into bottom and side of pie plate. Bake in 350-degree oven for 8 minutes, then cool. Sprinkle pecans over crust.

Filling

32 lge. marshmallows	1/2 tsp. allspice
1/2 c. milk	1 tbsp. melted butter
1 c. cooked mashed pumpkin	1 c. heavy cream, whipped
1/2 tsp. cinnamon	

Combine the marshmallows and milk in a saucepan and place over low heat until marshmallows are melted. Remove from heat and stir in pumpkin, cinnamon, allspice and butter. Fold in the whipped cream and pour into graham cracker crust. Chill for 3 hours.

Mrs. Russell B. Hall, West Palm Beach, Florida

RAISIN CREAM PIE

1 1/2 c. raisins	3 tbsp. cornstarch
2/3 c. sugar	1/2 c. cream
1/8 tsp. salt	1 baked pie shell
2 eggs, separated	1 recipe meringue

Combine the raisins and 1 cup water in a saucepan and simmer for 10 minutes. Add the sugar and salt and stir until the sugar is dissolved. Combine the beaten egg yolks, cornstarch and cream, then beat until well blended. Add to the raisin mixture and simmer, stirring constantly, until thickened. Pour into the pie shell and top with meringue. Bake at 375 degrees until browned.

Mrs. Everett Basham, Rising Sun, Maryland

RAISIN-LEMON PIE

1 c. raisins	1/4 c. lemon juice
1 c. sugar	1 tsp. grated lemon peel
1/4 tsp. salt	1 tbsp. butter
3 egg yolks	1 baked 9-in. pastry shell
2 tbsp. cornstarch	

Combine the raisins, 1 3/4 cups water and sugar in a saucepan and simmer for 10 minutes or until raisins are plump. Beat the salt, egg yolks and cornstarch together, then add to the raisin mixture and cook, stirring, until thickened. Add the lemon juice, peel and butter. Cool thoroughly and pour into the pie shell.

Meringue

3 egg whites	1/2 c. coconut
6 tbsp. sugar	

Beat the 3 egg whites until soft peaks form, then add the sugar gradually, beating until stiff peaks form. Fold in the coconut. Top pie with meringue. Bake at 325 degrees until lightly browned.

Mrs. F. W. Remington, Covington, Oklahoma

FRENCH STRAWBERRY PIE

1 8-oz. package cream cheese	1 baked 9-in. pie shell
1 1/2 c. sugar	1 1/2 pt. fresh strawberries
1/4 c. lemon juice	Whipped cream

Combine the cream cheese, 1/2 cup sugar and lemon juice, then cream until smooth. Spread over the pie shell. Mix the strawberries with remaining sugar until berries are well coated. Pour the strawberries over the filling and top with whipped cream.

Mrs. Staley Wood, Sparta, North Carolina

STRAWBERRY-APPLESAUCE PIE

1 pt. fresh California
  strawberries
1 c. heavy cream
2 tbsp. brown sugar
1/4 c. apricot preserves

1 9-in. gingersnap crumb
  crust
1 1/2 c. canned applesauce,
  chilled

Cut 4 or 5 strawberries in half and reserve for garnish, then slice the remaining strawberries. Whip the cream with the brown sugar until soft peaks form. Spread the preserves over bottom of pie crust. Add a layer of strawberries, then 1 cup of the applesauce. Spread the whipped cream on top, and mound the remaining applesauce in center of pie. Garnish with the reserved strawberry halves.

STRAWBERRY ICEBOX PIE

2 c. sliced fresh strawberries
1 c. sugar
1 can sweetened condensed milk

1/2 c. lemon juice
1 c. whipping cream, whipped
1 baked pie shell

Mix the strawberries and sugar, then chill for about 1 hour and drain. Combine the milk and lemon juice and mix until thickened. Fold half the whipped cream into the milk mixture, then fold in the strawberries. Pour into the pie shell and top with remaining whipped cream.

Shirley F. Banks, Minden, Louisiana

ANGEL FOOD STRAWBERRY PIE

1 pkg. frozen strawberries
3/4 c. sugar

Dash of salt
1/4 c. cornstarch

1/2 c. water
1 tsp. vanilla
1 c. heavy cream, whipped

1 baked pie shell
1/2 c. pecan halves

Thaw the strawberries. Mix the sugar, salt and cornstarch in a saucepan and stir in the water. Add the strawberries and cook over medium heat, stirring, until thick. Add vanilla and cool. Fold in the whipped cream and spoon into pie shell. Garnish with pecan halves.

Libby McLaughlin, Minter City, Mississippi

STRAWBERRY LEMON CURD PIE

1/4 c. butter
3 egg yolks
1 egg
5/8 c. sugar
1/2 c. lemon juice

1 tbsp. grated lemon peel
1 baked 9-in. pie shell
1 c. heavy cream
2 pt. fresh California
   strawberries, halved

Melt the butter in a saucepan. Beat the egg yolks and whole egg with 1/2 cup sugar until blended, then stir in the lemon juice and butter. Pour mixture into a saucepan and cook, stirring constantly, over low heat for 5 minutes or until thick as pudding. Stir in the lemon peel and cool. Spread a thin layer of the lemon mixture over the bottom of pie shell, then chill for about 30 minutes. Whip the cream with the remaining sugar until soft peaks form, then blend a small amount of the whipped cream with the remaining lemon curd. Fold in the remaining whipped cream. Reserve several strawberries for garnish. Place the remaining strawberry halves over lemon filling in pie shell, then cover with lemon cream. Chill for 3 or 4 hours. Garnish with the reserved strawberries.

STRAWBERRY CREAM PIE

1 pkg. vanilla pudding and pie
    filling mix
2 c. milk
1 baked pie shell

1 1/2 c. sliced sweetened
    strawberries
Whipped cream

Combine the pudding mix and milk in a saucepan. Bring to a boil over medium heat, stirring until thickened. Cool for about 5 minutes, stirring occasionally. Pour half the filling mixture into pie shell, then arrange the strawberries over filling. Cover with remaining filling. Chill for about 3 hours. Spread with whipped cream. Garnish with coconut and additional strawberries.

Mrs. C. L. Devine, Marshallberg, North Carolina

STRAWBERRY-GLAZED CHEESE PIE

1 1/4 c. graham cracker crumbs
1/4 c. melted butter
1 8-oz. package cream cheese
1/4 c. sugar
1 pkg. dessert topping mix

1 3-oz. package strawberry
    gelatin
1 10-oz. package frozen
    strawberries

Combine the crumbs and butter and mix thoroughly, then press firmly into pie pan. Chill. Mix the cream cheese with the sugar in a small bowl. Prepare the dessert topping mix according to package directions, beating until very stiff, then add to the cheese mixture. Spread a thin layer of the cheese mixture over crust, then mound remaining cheese mixture 2 inches around edge, leaving depression in center. Dissolve the gelatin in 1 cup boiling water, then add the strawberries. Chill until partially set, then spoon into center of pie. Chill for 3 hours.

Mrs. Lola Hopkins, Mardela, Maryland

STRAWBERRY-BANANA PIE

1/2 c. sugar
1/3 tsp. salt
1/4 c. cornstarch
1 c. strawberry syrup
2 tsp. lemon juice

1 tsp. red food coloring
1 baked pie shell
1 1/2 bananas, diced
1 c. drained strawberries
1 c. whipping cream, whipped

Combine the sugar, salt and cornstarch in a saucepan, then stir in the syrup. Bring to a boil, then reduce heat and cook, stirring, until thickened and clear. Stir in the lemon juice and food coloring. Line the pie shell with the sliced bananas, then cover with strawberries. Pour glaze over top and cool thoroughly. Top with whipped cream to serve.

Pam Sims, Waldron, Arkansas

RASPBERRY CREAM ANGEL PIE

1 10-oz. package frozen red raspberries in quick-thaw pouch	1/8 tsp. salt
	3 egg yolks, beaten
2 tsp. unflavored gelatin	3 tbsp. cognac or kirsch
1 1/2 c. heavy cream	Red food coloring (opt.)
1/2 c. sugar	1 baked 9-in. Meringue Shell, cooled

Thaw the raspberries according to package directions, then press through a fine sieve and discard seeds. Soften the gelatin in 1/4 cup cold water. Blend 1/2 cup of the cream, sugar and salt in a saucepan, then cook over medium heat until foamy. Blend a small amount of the hot mixture into the egg yolks, stirring rapidly, then return mixture to remaining hot mixture, stirring constantly. Cook over low heat for 1 minute, stirring constantly. Remove from heat and add gelatin, stirring until dissolved. Blend in the raspberries and cognac. Chill until mixture begins to thicken. Whip the remaining cream until stiff peaks form, then fold into the raspberry mixture. Add several drops of red food coloring. Spoon into the Meringue Shell. Chill for about 3 hours or until firm. Garnish with additional whipped cream and raspberries.

Meringue Shell

2 egg whites	1/2 c. sugar
1/8 tsp. salt	1/2 tsp. vanilla
1/8 tsp. cream of tartar	

Combine the egg whites, salt and cream of tartar and beat until foamy. Add the sugar, 2 tablespoons at a time, beating thoroughly after each addition until stiff peaks form. Add the vanilla and mix well. Spread the meringue mixture on bottom and side of a 9-inch pie pan. Bake at 250 degrees for 40 minutes, then turn off oven and cool for 60 minutes or overnight in oven.

RASPBERRY ALASKA PIE

1 2/3 c. graham cracker crumbs	1 tbsp. grated lemon rind
3/4 c. sugar	1/4 c. lemon juice
1/4 c. flaked coconut	1 qt. vanilla ice cream
1/4 c. soft margarine	4 egg whites
2 10-oz. packages frozen	1/8 tsp. salt
raspberries, thawed	1/4 c. flaked coconut
1 tbsp. cornstarch	

Combine the crumbs, 1/4 cup sugar, coconut and margarine and blend thoroughly. Place in a 9-inch pie plate and press firmly against bottom and side to form crust. Bake at 375 degrees for 7 minutes. Cool thoroughly. Drain the raspberries and reserve the syrup. Combine the cornstarch, lemon rind, lemon juice, reserved syrup and half the raspberries in a saucepan, then cook over medium heat, stirring constantly, until thickened. Remove from heat and cool thoroughly. Arrange the ice cream and half the sauce in alternate layers in the crust, then place in the freezer and freeze until firm. Combine the egg whites and salt and beat until foamy, then add the remaining sugar gradually, beating until stiff peaks form. Spread over the ice cream, sealing to crust edge. Sprinkle with coconut and return to freezer until ready to serve. Combine the remaining sauce with remaining raspberries for sauce. Preheat oven to 500 degrees then remove pie from freezer. Bake for about 3 minutes or until meringue is browned. Serve immediately with sauce.

Delores Ann Thorne, Metairie, Louisiana

LEMON ICE CREAM PIE

1 lge. can evaporated milk	Juice of 5 lemons
5 eggs, separated	3 vanilla wafer crumb crusts
1/2 c. sugar	

Chill the milk in the freezer for about 30 minutes. Combine the lightly beaten egg yolks, sugar and lemon juice and mix well. Beat the egg whites until stiff peaks form, then beat the milk with mixer until fluffy. Fold the egg whites and milk into the egg yolk mixture. Turn into the crumb crusts. Garnish tops with vanilla wafer crumbs. Freeze for several hours. May be stored in freezer for several months if wrapped in foil after frozen.

Mrs. Jack Horrocks, Texarkana, Texas

APPLESAUCE-ICE CREAM PIE

1 qt. vanilla ice cream	1 cinnamon-graham cracker crust
1 c. sweetened applesauce	

Place the ice cream in a bowl and stir to soften slightly. Add the applesauce and swirl through ice cream with a knife for a marble effect. Pour into the crust and freeze.

Hazel Wimer, Hightown, Virginia

FROZEN GRASSHOPPER PIE

1 1/2 c. chocolate cookie
    crumbs
1/4 c. melted butter
1/4 c. (packed) brown sugar
1 egg white
Dash of salt

2 tbsp. sugar
1/3 c. light corn syrup
1 c. heavy cream
4 tbsp. green creme de menthe
4 tbsp. white creme de cacao

Combine the crumbs, butter and brown sugar and mix well. Press into a 9-inch pie pan. Bake at 400 degrees for 5 minutes. Cool. Beat the egg white and salt together until soft peaks form. Add the sugar gradually, beating until smooth and glossy. Beat in the syrup slowly until stiff peaks form. Whip the cream until stiff, then fold in creme de menthe and creme de cacao. Fold the cream mixture into egg white mixture. Turn in pie crust and freeze overnight.

Mrs. William Edward Robinson, Jr., Milledgeville, Georgia

CHOCOLATE-MARSHMALLOW PIE

2 c. chocolate chip macaroon
    crumbs
1/4 c. butter or margarine,
    softened
1/4 c. sugar

1 qt. chocolate ice cream
1 c. marshmallow creme
2 tbsp. water
1/4 c. walnut halves

Blend the crumbs, butter and sugar together, then press firmly against bottom and side of a 9-inch pie plate. Bake at 375 degrees for 5 minutes. Cool, then freeze for 1 hour or longer. Soften the ice cream slightly, then pack into the pie shell. Freeze for several hours. Mix the marshmallow creme with the water and spoon over the pie just before serving, then sprinkle with the walnut halves. Allow to stand at room temperature for several minutes before serving.

PINEAPPLE-PECAN PIE

1 lge. can evaporated milk	1 pkg. black cherry gelatin
3 eggs, lightly beaten	1 c. chopped pecans
1 c. sugar	2 graham cracker crusts
1 sm. can crushed pineapple	2 c. whipped cream

Chill the milk in an ice tray in freezer until ice crystals form around edge. Combine the eggs, sugar and pineapple in a double boiler and cook, stirring constantly, until thick. Add the gelatin and stir until the gelatin is dissolved. Beat the milk until stiff peaks form, then fold in the gelatin mixture and pecans. Turn into the crusts. Spread the whipped cream over top. Freeze for several hours.

Mrs. J. D. Settle, Danville, Arkansas

CLOISTER FROZEN RUM PIE

4 c. graham cracker crumbs	1/4 c. rum
3/4 c. sugar	2 tbsp. lemon juice
1/4 c. melted butter	1/2 c. fine cake crumbs
3 eggs, at room temperature	2 c. heavy cream, whipped
1 env. unflavored gelatin	2 tbsp. brandy
2 tbsp. water	

Mix the graham cracker crumbs, 1/4 cup sugar and butter in a bowl. Place in two 9-inch pie pans and press firmly. Bake at 350 degrees until lightly browned. Place the eggs and remaining sugar in a bowl and beat well. Mix the gelatin, water, half the rum and lemon juice. Place over hot water and stir until gelatin is dissolved. Stir into egg mixture. Mix the cake crumbs with the whipped cream and blend into egg mixture. Add remaining rum and brandy and mix well. Place in graham cracker crusts and freeze for 10 to 12 hours. Remove from freezer several minutes before serving.

Mrs. William Barlow, Gallup, New Mexico

PUMPKIN PARTY PIE

1 1/2 pt. butter-pecan ice cream	1/4 tsp. salt
	1/4 tsp. nutmeg
1 c. pumpkin	1 tsp. cinnamon
1 c. sugar	1 c. whipped cream

Press the ice cream in a pie plate to form a shell, then place in freezer. Combine the pumpkin, sugar and spices in a saucepan and cook for 3 minutes. Cool to lukewarm, then fold in the whipped cream. Pour into the ice cream shell and freeze for several hours.

Mrs. George Worley, Little Rock, Arkansas

FROZEN PUMPKIN PIE

1 1/2 c. gingersnap cookie crumbs	1/3 c. (packed) light brown sugar
1/4 c. butter, melted	1 c. miniature marshmallows
1 egg	1 tsp. pumpkin pie spice
1/4 c. sugar	1 c. canned pumpkin
1/2 c. orange juice	1 c. evaporated milk, partially frozen

Combine the crumbs and butter in a foil-lined 9-inch pie plate. Press the crumbs evenly on bottom and side of plate to form crust. Freeze until filling is ready. Beat the egg well in a medium-sized saucepan, then stir in the sugar and orange juice. Cook over low heat, stirring constantly, until thickened. Add the brown sugar and marshmallows and stir until dissolved. Blend in pumpkin pie spice and pumpkin. Chill. Whip the evaporated milk in the small bowl of electric mixer until stiff peaks form. Fold in the chilled pumpkin mixture. Turn into crumb crust. Freeze for 8 hours or until firm.

Photograph for this recipe on page 34.

PISTACHIO ICE CREAM PIE

1 1/2 c. cold milk	1 c. heavy cream, whipped
1 pkg. instant pistachio pudding mix	1 baked 9-in. pie shell, cooled

Place the milk in a small mixing bowl, then add the pudding mix. Beat with an egg beater for about 1 minute or until well blended. Pour the pudding into a freezer tray, then place in freezer and freeze for about 30 to 45 minutes or until crystals form around the edges. Beat until smooth, then fold in the whipped cream. Pour into the pie shell and freeze until firm. Garnish with whipped cream swirls.

custard pies

One of the all-time family favorite pies is custard pie — any custard pie! The smooth mixtures of custards — eggs, milk, sugar, and flavorings — when baked in a pie shell emerge from your oven ready to bring praise from all who enjoy custard pie. *Southern Living* homemakers take pleasure in making these pies — and now they share that enjoyment with you in the recipes you'll find here.

As you turn the pages of this section, you'll find an almost-classic recipe for Coosa Shoofly Pie, a pie so much a part of the South that it was even featured in one of the region's popular songs! Look, too, at the recipe for Brandied Pumpkin Pie — it's particularly popular around Thanksgiving and Christmas when it adds a festive note to holiday dining tables. There's even a recipe for Chess Pie, an old English favorite featured in modern guise.

Every recipe in this section is the home-tested, family-approved favorite of the homemaker who shares it with you. She has spent hours in her kitchen, working and reworking the recipe until the blending of flavors is just right. It is her best recipe — and her signature on it is like a guarantee of picture-perfect pies, every time.

Earn welcome praise from everyone in your family — cap your next supper with a rich and delicious custard pie prepared with one of these recipes! It will be a treat you'll long remember!

AMBER PIE

1/2 c. sugar	1 tsp. lemon extract
2 tsp. flour	2 tbsp. buttermilk
1/4 tsp. salt	2 tbsp. melted butter
2 lge. eggs, lightly beaten	1 unbaked pie shell
1/2 c. sour cream	1 c. blackberry jam

Combine the sugar, flour and salt in a mixing bowl, then stir in the eggs and sour cream. Add the lemon extract, buttermilk and butter and mix well. Turn into the pie shell. Bake at 425 degrees for 10 minutes, then reduce the oven temperature to 350 degrees and bake for 30 minutes longer. Spread the jam over top and cool.

Mrs. K. C. Spaulding, Jonesboro, Tennessee

AMISH VANILLA PIE

1 c. sugar	1 c. (packed) brown sugar
1 c. molasses	1 tsp. cream of tartar
2 1/4 c. flour	1 tsp. soda
1 egg, well beaten	1/4 c. butter
2 c. water	1/4 c. shortening
1 tsp. vanilla	2 unbaked 9-in. pie shells

Combine the sugar, molasses, 1/4 cup flour, egg, water and vanilla in a saucepan and bring to a boil, stirring constantly. Set aside to cool. Combine the remaining flour, brown sugar, cream of tartar, soda, butter and shortening and mix with a fork until crumbly. Pour the molasses mixture into the pie shells and top with the crumb mixture. Bake at 350 degrees for about 40 minutes or until firm.

Arline Richcreek, Warner Robins, Georgia

APPLE-COTTAGE CHEESE PIE

2 eggs	1 c. cottage cheese
3/4 c. sugar	1 1/2 c. thinly sliced apples
1/8 tsp. salt	1/4 tsp. cinnamon
1/2 c. coffee cream, scalded	1/4 tsp. nutmeg
3/4 c. milk	1 unbaked 9-in. pie shell
1 tsp. vanilla	

Beat the eggs slightly, then add 1/2 cup sugar, salt, coffee cream, milk, vanilla and cottage cheese, blending well. Mix the apples with the remaining sugar, cinnamon and nutmeg, then turn into the pie shell. Bake at 425 degrees for 15 minutes. Reduce oven temperature to 325 degrees, then add the custard mixture. Bake for 40 minutes longer or until set and golden brown.

Mrs. R. M. Leonard, Midland, Virginia

APPLE-COCONUT PIE

3 c. thinly sliced tart apples
1/2 c. flaked coconut
1 unbaked 9-in. pie shell
1 egg

1 c. sugar
1/4 c. melted butter
2 tbsp. lemon juice

Combine the apples and coconut and place in the pie shell. Beat the egg well and add the remaining ingredients, mixing well. Pour over apples and coconut. Bake at 350 degrees for 45 to 50 minutes.

Mrs. James L. Morgan, Park Hill, Oklahoma

COUNTRY CREAM CHERRY PIE

1 No. 2 can cherry pie filling
1/2 c. ground almonds
1 c. sour cream
1 egg, beaten

1/2 tsp. almond extract
1/8 tsp. cinnamon
1 unbaked 8-in. pastry shell
1 tbsp. sugar

Combine the cherry pie filling, almonds, 1/2 cup sour cream, egg, almond extract and cinnamon and mix well. Pour into the pastry shell. Bake at 375 degrees for 45 minutes, then cool thoroughly. Combine the remaining sour cream and sugar and force through a pastry tube or spoon around edges of baked pie.

CLASSIC CHESS PIE

2 eggs
1 c. sugar
1 tbsp. cornmeal
1 tbsp. flour
3/4 c. milk or cream

1/3 c. melted butter
1/2 tsp. vinegar
1 tsp. vanilla
1 unbaked pie shell

Beat the eggs in a mixing bowl, then add the sugar, cornmeal and flour and stir. Add the milk, butter, vinegar and vanilla and mix. Pour into the pie shell. Bake at 375 degrees for 40 to 50 minutes or until custard is set and pastry browned.

Denise Russell, Hendersonville, Tennessee

SHOOFLY PIE

1 1/2 c. flour
1/2 c. (packed) brown sugar
1/4 tsp. salt
1/4 tsp. cinnamon
1/8 tsp. cloves
1/8 tsp. ginger
1/8 tsp. nutmeg

1/4 c. corn oil margarine
1 c. boiling water
1/2 c. dark molasses
1 1/2 tsp. soda
1 egg, slightly beaten
1 unbaked 8-in. pastry shell

Combine the flour, brown sugar, salt, cinnamon, cloves, ginger and nutmeg in a large bowl. Cut in the margarine with a pastry blender or 2 knives until mixture resembles coarse meal. Combine the water, molasses and soda, then blend in egg. Arrange alternate layers of crumbs and molasses mixture in the pastry shell, beginning and ending with crumbs. Bake at 450 degrees for 10 minutes. Reduce temperature to 350 degrees and bake for 15 minutes longer.

COOSA SHOOFLY PIE

1/2 tsp. soda	1/8 tsp. mace
1/2 c. molasses	1/8 tsp. ginger
1 egg yolk, well beaten	1/8 tsp. cloves
1 unbaked pie shell, chilled	1/2 c. (packed) brown sugar
3/4 c. flour	2 tbsp. shortening, melted
1/2 tsp. cinnamon	1/2 tsp. salt

Preheat oven to 400 degrees. Dissolve the soda in 1/4 cup hot water, then beat into the molasses. Blend in the egg yolk and pour into the pie shell. Combine the flour, spices, brown sugar, shortening and salt and blend with a fork until crumbly. Sprinkle over the pie. Bake for 10 minutes. Reduce temperature to 325 degrees and bake until firm.

Mrs. Lessie Barclay, Fayette, Alabama

HOLIDAY CHOCOLATE-PECAN PIE

2 sq. unsweetened chocolate	1 tsp. vanilla
3 tbsp. butter	1 c. coarsely chopped pecans
3/4 c. sugar	1 unbaked 9-in. pie shell
1 c. light corn syrup	1/2 c. whipping cream, whipped
3 eggs, slightly beaten	

Melt the chocolate and butter over hot water. Combine the sugar and syrup in saucepan and bring to a boil over high heat, stirring until sugar is dissolved. Boil for 1 minute. Pour the chocolate mixture slowly into the syrup, blending well, then pour very slowly over eggs, stirring constantly, to mix well. Add the vanilla and pecans, then pour into pie shell. Bake at 375 degrees for 45 to 50 minutes or until filling is puffed across top. Cool. Garnish with whipped cream and pecan halves before serving.

Mrs. Owen H. Link, Shreveport, Louisiana

GERMAN CHOCOLATE PIE

1/2 bar sweet cooking chocolate	1/4 c. milk
1/4 c. butter	1 1/2 tbsp. cornstarch
3/4 c. sugar	1 tsp. vanilla
Pinch of salt	1/2 c. chopped nuts
1/2 c. light corn syrup	1/4 c. flaked coconut
3 eggs	1 unbaked 9-in. pie shell

Melt the chocolate in top of double boiler over hot water. Add the butter, sugar, salt and corn syrup and stir until dissolved. Cool. Beat the eggs, then add the milk and cornstarch and mix well. Add to the chocolate mixture, then stir in the vanilla, nuts and coconut. Pour into the pie shell. Bake at 375 degrees for about 30 minutes or until filling is set.

Mrs. Arnold Smith, Chapel Hill, North Carolina

CHOCOLATE CUSTARD PIE

1 1/4 c. sugar	2 sq. chocolate, melted
6 tbsp. margarine	1/2 tsp. vanilla
3 eggs	1 unbaked 8-in. pie shell

Cream 1 cup sugar and margarine, then add 1 egg and 2 yolks, one at a time, beating well after each addition. Add the chocolate and vanilla, then turn into the pie shell. Bake at 350 degrees for 30 to 40 minutes. Beat the remaining egg whites until soft peaks form, then add the remaining sugar gradually, beating until stiff peaks form. Spread over the pie, sealing to the edges. Bake until browned.

Mrs. J. O. Kelly, Sr., Huntsville, Alabama

COCONUT MACAROON PIE

1 pkg. pie crust mix	2 tbsp. butter or margarine
1/4 tsp. salt	1 tsp. lemon juice
3 eggs, separated	1/4 tsp. almond extract
1 1/2 c. sugar	1 1/2 c. shredded coconut
1/4 c. milk	

Prepare the pie crust mix according to package directions. Line a 9-inch pie pan with the pastry and roll the remaining pastry 1/8 inch thick. Cut in long strips about 1/4 inch wide and braid 3 strips together, joining when necessary to make braid long enough to go around rim of pie. Moisten edge of pastry in pan and place braid loosely around edge. Add salt to egg yolks and beat until thick and lemon colored. Add the sugar, 1/2 cup at a time, beating well after each addition. Add the milk, butter, lemon juice and almond extract and blend well. Fold in the coconut and stiffly beaten egg whites, then turn into pie shell. Bake in 375-degree oven for 50 minutes or until knife inserted in center comes out clean. Cool. Garnish with whipped cream and toasted coconut, if desired.

Gladys Barrett, Richmond, Virginia

COCONUT CARAMEL PIE

3 eggs, beaten	3 tsp. vinegar
1 c. sugar	1 c. coconut
2 tbsp. brown sugar	1 tsp. vanilla
1 stick margarine, melted	1 unbaked 9-in. pie shell

Combine the eggs and sugars and mix well. Add the margarine, vinegar, coconut and vanilla and stir until well blended. Pour into the pie shell. Bake at 350 degrees for 30 to 45 minutes.

Mrs. M. E. Johnson, Flippen, Georgia

CLASSIC CUSTARD PIE

1 unbaked 9-in. pastry shell	1/2 tsp. vanilla
4 eggs, slightly beaten	1/8 tsp. almond extract
1/2 c. sugar	2 1/2 c. milk, scalded
1/4 tsp. salt	Nutmeg to taste

Chill the pie shell. Blend the eggs, sugar, salt, vanilla and almond extract, then stir in the milk gradually. Pour into the pie shell and sprinkle with nutmeg. Bake at 400 degrees for 25 to 30 minutes or until knife inserted halfway between outside and center of custard comes out clean. Cool on rack for 15 to 30 minutes, then chill in refrigerator.

Mary D. Blankenship, Oklahoma City, Oklahoma

DATE PIE

4 eggs, separated	1 tbsp. orange juice
Pinch of salt	2 tbsp. lemon juice
2 c. sugar	1/2 tsp. cinnamon
1 c. chopped dates	1/2 tsp. nutmeg
1 c. chopped pecans	2 unbaked 9-in. pie shells
2 tbsp. melted butter	

Beat the egg yolks with salt, then add the remaining ingredients except egg whites and pie shells. Fold in the stiffly beaten egg whites. Pour into shells. Bake at 350 degrees for about 40 minutes or until firm.

Mrs. Rubye Shepherd, Wills Point, Texas

HOLIDAY DATE PIE

1 1/2 c. chopped dates	1/2 tsp. nutmeg
1 unbaked 9-in. pie shell	1/4 tsp. cloves
1 1/2 c. cream or evaporated milk	1/2 tsp. salt
3 eggs	2 tbsp. dry bread crumbs
1 c. sugar	2 tsp. vanilla
1 1/2 tsp. cinnamon	3/4 c. shredded coconut

Place the dates in the pie shell. Combine the remaining ingredients except coconut in a bowl and beat with rotary beater. Pour over the dates. Bake at 450 degrees for 15 minutes. Reduce the temperature to 325 degrees, then sprinkle with the coconut. Bake for 30 to 35 minutes longer or until knife inserted 1 inch from edge comes out clean. Serve with cinnamon-flavored whipped cream, if desired.

Mrs. E. E. Chandler, Floresville, Texas

LEMON-LITE PIE

3 eggs, separated
3/4 c. sugar
2 tbsp. flour
1/4 tsp. salt
1/4 c. butter, melted

1 c. evaporated milk
1/3 c. lemon juice
2 tsp. grated lemon peel
Yellow food coloring (opt.)
1 unbaked 9-in. pastry shell

Preheat the oven to 400 degrees. Beat the egg yolks slightly in a large mixing bowl. Blend 1/2 cup sugar, flour and salt together, then stir into egg yolks. Add the butter, evaporated milk, lemon juice and peel, then stir in the food coloring. Beat the egg whites until frothy, then beat in the remaining sugar gradually, beating until stiff but not dry. Fold the lemon mixture into meringue lightly but thoroughly. Pour into the pastry shell. Bake for 10 minutes. Reduce temperature to 350 degrees and bake for 20 minutes longer. Cool and serve.

LEMON CAKE PIE

1 c. sugar
1/4 c. flour
1/4 c. margarine, melted
1/8 tsp. salt
2 eggs, separated

Juice and grated peel of 2 lemons
1 c. milk
1 unbaked 9-in. pie shell

Combine the sugar, flour, margarine, salt and egg yolks and beat until smooth. Beat in the lemon juice and peel. Add the milk slowly, beating constantly. Beat the egg whites until stiff but not dry, then fold into the milk mixture. Bake the pie shell at 350 degrees for 5 minutes, then pour in the filling. Bake for 40 minutes or until filling is firm.

Mrs. E. F. Jones, San Antonio, Texas

GLAZED BUTTERMILK PIE

1 c. sugar
1/4 c. flour
1/2 tsp. salt
1/4 tsp. mace or nutmeg
1/4 tsp. cinnamon
2 c. buttermilk

3 eggs, slightly beaten
1 unbaked pie shell
1 No. 303 can apricot halves
4 tsp. cornstarch
1/3 c. orange marmalade

Combine the sugar, flour, salt and spices in top of double boiler, then stir in the buttermilk and cook over boiling water, stirring constantly, until thickened. Beat 1/2 cup of the hot mixture into the eggs, then return to hot buttermilk mixture. Cook, stirring constantly, until thick. Bake the pie shell at 400 degrees for 5 minutes. Reduce oven temperature to 325 degrees. Pour the buttermilk mixture into the pie shell. Bake for 50 minutes to 1 hour or until filling is set. Cool on rack. Drain the apricots and reserve the syrup. Mix 1/4 cup reserved apricot syrup and cornstarch together until smooth. Bring the remaining syrup to a boil, then add the cornstarch mixture. Cook, stirring constantly, until mixture is clear and thick. Remove from heat and blend in the marmalade. Arrange apricot halves over pie filling and cover with the glaze.

Patricia Gawlik, Falls City, Texas

JAPANESE FRUIT PIE

2 eggs, beaten
1 c. sugar
1 stick butter, melted
1 tbsp. vinegar

1/2 c. flaked coconut
1/2 c. chopped pecans
1/2 c. raisins
1 unbaked pie shell

Combine the eggs and sugar, then blend in the butter and vinegar. Stir in the coconut, pecans and raisins. Turn into the pie shell. Bake at 300 degrees for 40 minutes.

Mrs. B. H. Gregory, Sr., Carlisle, South Carolina

MAPLE SYRUP PIE

3 tbsp. flour
1/2 c. sweet cream
2 egg yolks, lightly beaten
Pinch of salt

1 c. maple syrup
1 tsp. vanilla
1 unbaked 9-in. pie shell
1 recipe meringue

Mix the flour with the cream to make a smooth paste. Add the egg yolks, salt, syrup and vanilla and mix until smooth. Pour into the pie shell. Bake at 400 degrees for 35 to 40 minutes or until firm. Top with the meringue and bake until browned.

Mrs. J. R. Davis, Burkes Garden, Virginia

OATMEAL PIE

3 eggs, well beaten	2/3 c. quick-cooking oats
2/3 c. sugar	2/3 c. flaked coconut
1 c. (packed) brown sugar	1 tsp. vanilla
2 tbsp. butter	1 unbaked pie shell

Combine the eggs, sugars and butter and mix well. Stir in the oats, coconut and vanilla. Turn into the pie shell. Bake at 350 degrees for 30 to 35 minutes.

Mrs. R. F. Poehlmann, Brenham, Texas

OSGOOD PIE

4 eggs, beaten	4 tsp. vinegar
2 c. sugar	1/2 c. butter
1 tbsp. cornstarch	1 tsp. vanilla
1 tsp. cinnamon	1 c. chopped pecans
Pinch of nutmeg	1 c. raisins
Pinch of salt	1 unbaked pastry shell

Combine the first 7 ingredients and beat well. Add the butter, vanilla, pecans and raisins. Pour into the pastry shell. Bake at 350 degrees for 50 minutes to 1 hour.

Maggie Bridgeman, Englehard, North Carolina

OZARK PIE

1/2 c. sifted flour	1 tsp. vanilla
2 tsp. baking powder	1 c. chopped walnuts
1/2 tsp. salt	1 c. finely chopped apples
2 eggs	1 unbaked 9-in. pie shell
1 c. (packed) brown sugar	

Combine the flour, baking powder and salt, then sift. Beat the eggs until light and lemon colored, then beat in the brown sugar gradually, beating until creamy. Stir in the flour mixture, vanilla, walnuts and apples and mix well. Spoon into the pie shell. Bake at 400 degrees for 15 minutes. Reduce temperature to 350 degrees and bake for 15 minutes longer or until filling is set. Cool and garnish with whipped cream before serving.

Mrs. Houston Hardin, Russellville, Alabama

PEANUT BUTTER PIE

2 eggs, slightly beaten	1/2 c. sugar
1/2 c. peanut butter	1 tbsp. flour

1 tbsp. margarine, softened
1 tsp. vanilla

1 c. corn syrup
1 unbaked pie shell

Combine the eggs and peanut butter and mix until well blended. Combine the sugar and flour and blend into the egg mixture. Add the margarine, vanilla and syrup and and mix until well combined. Turn into the pie shell. Bake at 425 degrees for 10 minutes. Reduce temperature to 350 degrees and bake for 1 hour longer.

Mrs. John McGregor, Knott, Texas

PERSIMMON PIE

2 eggs, slightly beaten
2 c. ripe persimmon pulp
3/4 c. sugar
1 tbsp. flour
1/2 tsp. salt

1/2 tsp. cinnamon
1/4 tsp. ginger
1/4 tsp. cloves
1 2/3 c. evaporated milk
1 unbaked 9-in. pie shell

Combine the eggs and persimmon pulp and stir until well blended. Combine the sugar, flour, salt and spices and blend into the persimmon mixture. Stir in the milk gradually, blending well. Pour into the pie shell. Bake at 425 degrees for 15 minutes. Reduce temperature to 350 degrees and bake for 45 minutes longer. Serve with whipped cream, if desired.

Mrs. Jack Arledge, De Ridder, Louisiana

PEACH DELIGHT PIE

3 egg yolks
3/4 c. sugar
1 can evaporated milk
1 tsp. vanilla

1/2 tsp. almond flavoring
2 c. mashed, cooked dried
   peaches, sweetened
1 unbaked pie shell

Beat the egg yolks thoroughly, then add the sugar and milk, beating well. Add the flavorings and peaches, then pour into the pie shell. Bake at 400 degrees for 15 minutes. Reduce the temperature to 350 degrees and bake for 25 minutes longer or until firm and browned.

Meringue

3 egg whites
2 tbsp. sugar

Pinch of cream of tartar

Beat the egg whites until soft peaks form, then add the sugar and cream of tartar gradually, beating until stiff peaks form. Spread on the pie and brown lightly.

Mrs. E. K. Bullock, Landrum, South Carolina

PEACH-PECAN PIE

3 eggs, beaten
1 No. 2 can peach pie filling
1/4 tsp. salt
1 c. dark corn syrup

1 c. pecan halves
1 tsp. vanilla
1 unbaked 10-in. pie shell

Combine the eggs, pie filling and salt, then add the corn syrup, pecans and vanilla. Pour into the pie shell. Bake at 425 degrees for 10 minutes. Reduce the temperature to 325 degrees and bake for 45 to 50 minutes longer or until set.

PINEAPPLE CHESS PIE

2 c. sugar
1 tbsp. cornmeal
2 tbsp. flour
1/4 c. butter, melted

4 eggs, well beaten
1/2 c. flaked coconut
1 sm. can crushed pineapple
1 unbaked pie shell

Combine the sugar, cornmeal and flour, then stir in the butter and eggs, mixing well. Fold in the coconut and pineapple and turn into the pie shell. Bake at 300 degrees for 45 minutes.

Jessie Reiser, Shawnee, Oklahoma

EASY PINEAPPLE PIE

2 c. sugar
3 tbsp. flour
5 egg yolks
1 c. buttermilk

1 c. crushed pineapple
1 tsp. vanilla
2 tbsp. melted butter
2 unbaked 9-in. pie shells

Sift the sugar and flour together. Beat the egg yolks until light, then add the sugar mixture and beat well. Blend in the buttermilk, then add the pineapple, vanilla and butter and mix well. Pour into the pie shells. Bake at 325 degrees until filling is set and browned.

Mrs. Bob Durham, Dallas, Texas

PINEAPPLE-COCONUT PIE

1/4 lb. butter	1 sm. can crushed pineapple,
2 c. sugar	drained
4 eggs, beaten	2 unbaked 8-in. pie shells
1 sm. can coconut	

Cream the butter with the sugar, then add the eggs and mix well. Blend in the coconut and pineapple. Pour into the pie shell. Bake at 350 degrees for 30 to 40 minutes or until firm.

Mrs. George Mosley, Union, South Carolina

PINTO BEAN PIE

3 eggs	1/4 tsp. salt
1 1/2 c. sugar	1 tsp. baking powder
1 c. milk	2 c. cooked mashed pinto
1 tsp. vanilla	beans
1/4 c. melted butter	1 unbaked 9-in. pie shell
1/2 c. flour	

Beat the eggs with the sugar, then blend in the milk, vanilla and butter. Combine the flour, salt and baking powder and stir into the egg mixture until well blended. Blend in the beans and turn into the pie shell. Bake at 350 degrees until firm.

Mrs. Mary S. Ross, Haworth, Oklahoma

SOUR CREAM-PRUNE PIE

1 1/2 c. prunes	Dash of salt
1 c. sugar	1/4 tsp. nutmeg
2 eggs	1 unbaked 9-in. pastry shell
1 c. sour cream	

Snip the prunes from the pits with scissors. Beat the sugar and eggs together until light and foamy, then beat in the sour cream, salt, nutmeg and prunes. Turn into the pastry shell. Bake in 450-degree oven for 10 minutes. Reduce the temperature to 350 degrees and bake for 20 minutes longer or until golden brown. Garnish with whipped cream and cooked, plump prunes, if desired.

Mrs. Mary Davidson, Avondale, North Carolina

PLUM JELLY PIE

3 eggs	1/2 c. cream
1/2 c. sugar	1/2 tsp. vanilla
1 tbsp. flour	1/4 tsp. salt
1/4 c. butter or margarine	1 unbaked 9-in. pie shell
1/4 c. red plum jelly	

Beat the eggs until light. Combine the sugar and flour and beat into the eggs. Combine the butter and jelly in a small saucepan and melt over low heat, then add to egg mixture gradually, beating constantly until well blended. Add the cream, vanilla and salt and mix well. Turn into the pie shell. Bake at 450 degrees for 10 minutes. Reduce temperature to 350 degrees and bake for 40 minutes longer or until filling is set.

Mrs. Franklin Gaynor, Hawesville, Kentucky

BEST-EVER PUMPKIN PIE

1/2 c. margarine or butter	1 c. (packed) brown sugar
3 c. cooked mashed pumpkin	4 egg yolks, beaten
Pinch of salt	1/2 c. chopped pecans
1/2 c. syrup	1/2 c. chopped raisins
1/4 tsp. allspice	1/2 c. chopped maraschino cherries
1/4 tsp. cloves	1 unbaked 9-in. pie crust
1 c. sugar	

Melt the margarine in a saucepan and add the pumpkin, salt, syrup, spices and sugars. Cook for about 10 minutes, stirring, then stir in egg yolks. Cook for about 15 minutes longer, stirring frequently. Add pecans, raisins and cherries and place in pie crust. Bake at 400 degrees for about 40 minutes.

Mrs. Sam Lassiter, Sr., Gadsden, Alabama

PUMPKIN PIE WITH PECAN TOPPING

1 1-lb. 13-oz. can pumpkin	1/4 tsp. cloves
1 c. (packed) brown sugar	4 eggs, slightly beaten
1 c. sugar	2 c. milk, scalded
2 tbsp. molasses	2 unbaked 9-in. pie shells
1 tsp. salt	1 c. pecan halves
3 tsp. cinnamon	

Combine the pumpkin, sugars, molasses, salt and spices and mix well. Blend in the eggs, then add the hot milk gradually, stirring constantly. Pour half the mixture into each pie shell. Bake at 400 degrees for 10 minutes. Reduce oven temperature to 350 degrees and bake for 30 minutes longer or until crust is done and filling is set. Top with pecan halves before serving.

Photograph for this recipe on page 64.

BRANDIED PUMPKIN PIE

3 eggs, separated	1/2 tsp. ground cloves
1/2 c. brown sugar	1/2 tsp. ginger
1/2 c. sugar	1 1/2 c. pumpkin
3 tbsp. dark corn syrup	1 1/2 c. milk
3 tbsp. cornstarch	1 tbsp. brandy
1/4 tsp. salt	1 unbaked 9-in. pie shell
1 tsp. cinnamon	

Beat egg whites to soft peak stage and set aside. Beat the egg yolks and stir in the sugars, syrup, cornstarch, salt and spices until well mixed. Add the pumpkin and liquids and mix well. Fold in the egg whites and pour into the pie shell. Bake at 425 degrees for 10 minutes. Reduce temperature to 350 degrees and bake for 35 minutes or until silver knife inserted near center comes out clean. Serve with whipped cream.

Mrs. Clayton Williams, Dover, Delaware

HARVEST PUMPKIN PIE

1 c. (packed) brown sugar	1/2 c. cream or evaporated
1/2 tsp. salt	milk
1/2 tsp. ginger	1 tbsp. angostura aromatic
1 tsp. cinnamon	bitters
2 eggs, slightly beaten	1 1/2 c. cooked pumpkin
1 1/2 c. milk	1 unbaked pie shell

Mix the brown sugar, salt and spices, then add the eggs, milk, cream, bitters and pumpkin. Mix well and pour into the pie shell. Bake at 425 degrees for 40 to 45 minutes or until knife inserted comes out clean. Garnish with whipped cream.

FANCY PUMPKIN PIE

1 c. flour	3 eggs
1/3 tsp. salt	1/2 c. milk
1/3 c. shortening	1 No. 303 can pumpkin
1 c. sugar	1/2 tsp. cinnamon
1/4 c. butter or margarine	1/4 tsp. allspice

Sift the flour and salt together, then blend in shortening until well mixed. Add just enough cold water to make a pliable dough. Roll out and line a deep 9-inch pie plate. Cream the sugar and butter, then add eggs and beat well. Stir in the milk and mix well. Add the pumpkin and spices and mix thoroughly. Pour into the prepared crust. Bake at 400 degrees until crust begins to brown. Reduce temperature to 250 degrees and bake until filling is set and crust is golden brown.

Mrs. E. J. Olson, Walnut Springs, Texas

PUMPKIN PIE WITH MINCEMEAT

1 1/2 c. cooked pumpkin	1/4 tsp. nutmeg
1 c. evaporated milk	1 tbsp. butter
1 c. sugar	2 eggs, slightly beaten
1/4 tsp. salt	1 unbaked pie crust
1/4 tsp. cinnamon	1 c. hot moist mincemeat

Combine all ingredients except the pie crust and mincemeat in a bowl and mix thoroughly. Pour into the pie crust. Bake at 425 degrees for 15 minutes. Reduce temperature to 350 degrees and bake for 45 minutes longer or until knife inserted in center comes out clean. Top with mincemeat and garnish with whipped cream.

Mrs. Eleanor Stone, Staunton, Virginia

SORGHUM MOLASSES CUSTARD

2 eggs	1 tbsp. melted butter
1/2 c. sugar	1 tsp. orange juice
1/2 c. sorghum	1 unbaked pie shell

Beat the eggs until thick and foamy, adding the sugar, gradually. Beat in the sorghum, butter and orange juice, then pour into the pie shell. Bake at 325 degrees for 30 minutes or until custard is set.

Mrs. Mack Earle, Christiana, Tennessee

SPICY SQUASH PIE

1 c. (packed) brown sugar	1/8 tsp. each cloves and nutmeg
1 tbsp. flour	1/8 tsp. each cinnamon and
1/2 tsp. salt	ginger

1/8 tsp. allspice

1 1/2 c. canned squash

1 egg, beaten

1 1/2 c. scalded milk

1 9-in. pie crust

Combine the brown sugar, flour, salt, spices and squash in a bowl and mix thoroughly. Add the egg and mix well. Stir in milk and pour into pie crust. Bake at 450 degrees for 30 to 40 minutes or until knife inserted in center comes out clean.

Mrs. R. L. Hunt, Winston-Salem, North Carolina

GOLDEN SQUASH PIE

1 c. (packed) brown sugar

3/4 tsp. salt

1 1/2 tsp. nutmeg

1 tsp. cinnamon

3/4 tsp. ginger

1/2 tsp. cloves

2 c. cooked squash, sieved

3 eggs, beaten

1/4 c. melted butter

1 1/2 c. milk

1 unbaked 9-in. pie shell

Combine the brown sugar, salt, spices and squash and mix thoroughly. Add the eggs, butter and milk to squash mixture and mix well, then pour into the pie shell. Bake at 450 degrees for 10 minutes. Reduce temperature to 350 degrees and bake for 40 minutes longer or until knife inserted in center comes out clean. Allow to cool slightly before serving. Serve with whipped cream.

SQUASH CUSTARD PIE

2 eggs	1 c. cooked mashed squash
Sugar	1 unbaked pie shell
1 c. milk	1 c. heavy cream
1 tsp. salt	1 tsp. vanilla
1 tsp. cinnamon	

Beat the eggs until foamy, then add 2/3 cup sugar, milk, salt, cinnamon and squash. Mix well with beater. Pour into the pie shell. Bake at 375 degrees until the custard sets and crust is browned. Cool. Whip the cream until fluffy, then add 1/4 cup sugar gradually, beating until stiff. Fold in the vanilla. Spread over pie just before serving.

Maude M. Hooks, Pantego, North Carolina

HONEY-PECAN PIE

1 stick butter	2 tbsp. cider vinegar
1 c. honey	1 tsp. vanilla
1 c. sugar	2 c. pecan halves
3 lge. eggs, beaten	1 unbaked 10-in. pie shell
1/2 tsp. salt	

Melt the butter in a saucepan over low heat, then add the honey, sugar, eggs, salt, vinegar and vanilla. Mix well. Arrange the pecans in the pie shell and pour the butter mixture over pecans. Bake at 350 degrees for 35 to 45 minutes.

Berta L. Lindbergh, Birmingham, Alabama

PECAN PIE

3/4 c. sugar	1 tsp. vinegar
1 c. dark corn syrup	1 tsp. vanilla
1 tbsp. flour	1/2 c. chopped pecans
2 tbsp. melted margarine	1 unbaked 8-in. pie shell
3 eggs	1/2 c. pecan halves

Combine the sugar, corn syrup, flour and margarine in a bowl and cream well. Beat in eggs, one at a time. Add vinegar and vanilla and mix well. Add chopped pecans and pour into pie shell. Top with pecan halves. Bake at 300 degrees for 20 minutes. Increase temperature to 350 degrees and bake for 20 minutes longer.

Mrs. Grady Coleman, Shreveport, Louisiana

PECAN-OATMEAL PIE

2 eggs, beaten	2/3 c. melted butter
3/4 c. sugar	2 tsp. vanilla
3/4 c. quick-cooking oatmeal	1 unbaked pie shell
3/4 c. dark corn syrup	2/3 c. pecan halves
2/3 c. coconut	

Combine all the ingredients except the pie shell and pecans and mix well. Turn into the pie shell. Bake at 300 degrees for 20 minutes. Arrange the pecans on top and bake for 20 minutes longer or until filling is set and crust is browned.

Mrs. Orlie Barnes, Kingsport, Tennessee

MOCK PECAN PIE

2 eggs, well beaten	1 c. (packed) brown sugar
3/4 c. quick-cooking oats	3/4 c. sugar
1 tsp. vanilla	2/3 c. grated coconut
2 tbsp. melted butter	1 unbaked pie shell

Combine all the ingredients except the pie shell and mix well. Turn into the pie shell. Bake at 350 degrees until firm.

Stella Vaughn, South Coffeyville, Oklahoma

SAMPLE PECAN PIE

3 eggs, slightly beaten	2 tbsp. melted corn oil
1 c. dark corn syrup	margarine
1 c. sugar	1 c. pecans
1 tsp. vanilla	1 unbaked 9-in. pastry
1/8 tsp. salt	shell

Mix the eggs, corn syrup, sugar, vanilla, salt and margarine thoroughly, then stir in the pecans. Pour into the pastry shell in pie pan. Bake at 400 degrees for 15 minutes. Reduce temperature to 350 degrees and bake for 30 to 35 minutes longer. Filling should be slightly less set in center than around edge.

PECAN-PUMPKIN PIE

3 eggs	2 tsp. pumpkin pie spices
1/2 c. sugar	1 1/2 c. mashed cooked
1/2 c. (packed) brown sugar	pumpkin
1 tbsp. flour	1 1/2 c. cream
1/2 tsp. salt	1 unbaked pie shell

Beat the eggs, then blend with the sugars, flour, salt and spices. Add the pumpkin and mix well. Stir in the cream until well blended, then pour into the pie shell. Bake at 450 degrees for 10 minutes.

Pecan Topping

1 tbsp. brown sugar	3/4 c. chopped pecans
2 tbsp. butter	

Melt the brown sugar and butter in a saucepan, then add the pecans. Spread on top of the pie. Reduce temperature to 350 degrees and bake for 40 to 45 minutes longer or until a knife inserted in filling comes out clean.

Mrs. R. T. Garville, Alamo, Georgia

LEMONY SWEET POTATO PIE

3 eggs, slightly beaten	1/4 c. lemon juice
1 c. (packed) brown sugar	2 tbsp. melted margarine
1 c. milk	1 1/2 c. mashed sweet potatoes
1 tsp. cinnamon	1/2 c. chopped pecans or
1/2 tsp. nutmeg	walnuts
1/2 tsp. ginger	1 unbaked pie shell
1/2 tsp. salt	

Combine the eggs, brown sugar, milk, cinnamon, nutmeg, ginger and salt and mix well. Add the lemon juice and margarine and beat with electric mixer or rotary beater. Blend in potatoes and pecans. Pour into the pie shell. Bake at 375 degrees for about 50 minutes to 1 hour or until knife inserted in pie comes out clean. Serve with whipped cream or ice cream.

Mrs. A. C. Johnson, Mt. Burg, Arkansas

BLACK WALNUT PIE

1/2 c. butter	1/8 tsp. salt
1 c. sugar	3 egg yolks
1/4 c. flour	1/2 c. evaporated milk

1 tsp. vanilla   2/3 c. chopped black walnuts
1 unbaked 9-in. pie shell

Cream the butter, adding the sugar gradually and beating until light and fluffy. Add the flour, salt and egg yolks and mix well. Stir in milk and vanilla, then pour into the pie shell. Sprinkle with the walnuts. Bake at 425 degrees for 10 minutes. Reduce temperature to 300 degrees and bake for 40 minutes longer or until set.

Mrs. Charles Lee, Tallahassee, Florida

FILBERT CARAMEL PIE

1 1/3 c. sifted all-purpose flour
3/4 tsp. salt
1/2 c. vegetable shortening
3 tbsp. water
3 eggs
1/2 c. (packed) dark brown
  sugar

1 c. light corn syrup
1 tsp. vanilla
1/2 c. butter or margarine,
  melted
1 1/2 c. chopped toasted
  filberts

Combine the flour and 1/2 teaspoon salt in a bowl, then cut in shortening until uniform but coarse. Sprinkle with the water and toss with a fork, then press into ball. Roll out pastry on lightly floured surface, 1 1/2 inches larger than inverted 9-inch pie plate. Fit into plate and trim 1/2 inch beyond edge of plate, folding under to make double thickness around edge. Flute or trim even with edge and decorate with small pastry cutouts. Beat the eggs, brown sugar, syrup, remaining salt and vanilla together, then stir in the butter and filberts. Pour into the pie shell. Bake at 375 degrees for 45 minutes or until set in center. Cool.

chiffon pies

Chiffon pies are everyone's delightful taste treat. The filling may be tart or sweet, but it is certain to just about melt in your mouth. Gelatin and cloud-light whipped cream mingle with beaten egg whites to create pies that finish almost every dinner or lunch with a very special flourish.

Southern families love chiffon pies and prize those which are piled high with delectably light fillings of all descriptions. To please their families, southern homemakers turn their considerable culinary skills to the making of just-perfect chiffon pies — and the result is the kind of recipes you'll find in this section.

Cap that extra-special dinner with Sherry-Almond Pie, a tantalizing blend of flavors certain to bring you admiring compliments — and requests for "that wonderful recipe!" Capitalize on palate-tingling, tangy fruit flavors, too, by preparing pies like Tangy Orange Chiffon Pie . . . Fresh Peach Angel Pie . . . or Apricot and Chiffon Pie. There's even a recipe for Peanut Brittle Pie.

There are home-tested recipes, the kind friends share with each other . . . the kind people used to collect, cherish, and carefully pass from one generation to another. It was recipes like these that constituted one of the most priceless heritages from the southern past. They are recipes from *Southern Living* homemakers—and they are yours in the section that follows.

APPLE BUTTER PUFF PIE

2 eggs, separated
1 c. spicy apple butter
1 tsp. lemon juice
2 tbsp. flour
1/2 tsp. salt

1/2 c. chopped prunes
2/3 c. scalded milk
1 baked pie shell
Marshmallows

Beat the egg yolks and combine with the apple butter, lemon juice, flour, salt and prunes in a double boiler. Add the milk gradually, stirring constantly. Cook, stirring constantly, over hot water until thick and smooth. Beat the egg whites until stiff and fold into apple butter mixture, then pour into the pie shell. Place a ring of marshmallows, set close together, around outer edge of pie. Place 1 marshmallow in the center. Bake at 400 degrees until marshmallows are browned.

Mrs. Lula Kirk, Pocahontas, Tennessee

APRICOT CHIFFON PIE

1 tsp. butter or margarine
1   3 1/2-oz. can flaked
    coconut
1 env. unflavored gelatin
1/3 c. sugar

Dash of salt
1   12-oz. can apricot nectar
1 tsp. lemon juice
1/8 tsp. almond extract
2 egg whites

Spread the butter evenly into bottom and up the side of a 9-inch pie plate. Empty the coconut into the pie plate and press against the bottom and side. Bake at 325 degrees for 10 minutes or until edges are golden brown, then cool. Mix the gelatin, sugar and salt thoroughly. Heat the apricot nectar just to boiling, then add to the gelatin mixture and stir until dissolved. Add the lemon juice and almond extract and chill until partially set. Add the egg whites and beat until soft peaks form. Pile into cooled coconut crust and chill until firm.

Mrs. J. H. Robinson, Jr., Alexander City, Alabama

CHERRY CHIFFON PIE

1 1/2 c. graham cracker crumbs
1/4 c. margarine
1   16-oz. can red sour
    cherries, drained
1/2 c. sugar

1   3-oz. package cherry
    gelatin
1/2 c. chopped walnuts
2/3 c. evaporated milk
1 tbsp. lemon juice

Mix the crumbs and margarine and press into a 9-inch pie pan. Bake at 350 degrees for 10 minutes, then cool. Cut the cherries in half. Dissolve the sugar and gelatin in 1 cup hot water, then chill to the consistency of unbeaten egg whites. Fold in the cherries and walnuts and chill for 10 minutes. Chill the milk in a refrigerator tray until soft crystals form around edges of tray. Whip until stiff, then add lemon juice and whip until stiff. Fold into the cherry mixture. Spoon into the pie shell and chill until firm. Garnish with walnut halves, if desired.

Mary Jane Brown, Memphis, Tennessee

MARASCHINO SOUFFLE PIE

1 8-oz. jar red maraschino
  cherries
1 8 1/4-oz. can crushed
  pineapple
1 env. unflavored gelatin
4 eggs, separated

2 tbsp. lemon juice
1/8 tsp. salt
1/2 c. sugar
1/2 c. heavy cream
Coconut Pie Shell

Drain the cherries and chop, then drain the pineapple and reserve the syrup. Add enough water to the pineapple syrup to make 3/4 cup liquid. Soften the gelatin in the pineapple liquid in a saucepan, then add the beaten egg yolks and blend thoroughly. Place over low heat and cook, stirring constantly, for about 5 minutes or until gelatin dissolves and mixture coats a metal spoon. Remove from heat and stir in the lemon juice and salt, then cool slightly. Add the cherries and pineapple. Beat the egg whites until soft peaks form and add the sugar gradually, beating until stiff but not dry. Fold into the gelatin mixture. Beat the cream until soft peaks form, then fold into the gelatin mixture. Turn into the pie shell and chill for about 4 hours. Garnish pie with whole cherries, if desired.

Coconut Pie Shell

1/2 c. butter

1 3 1/2-oz. can flaked coconut

Melt the butter in a large skillet over medium heat, then add the coconut and toss until evenly coated. Press mixture evenly and firmly on bottom and side of a 9-inch pie plate. Form a rim around side of plate. Cover side and rim of shell with strips of aluminum foil. Bake at 300 degrees for 20 minutes or until bottom of shell starts to brown. Remove the foil and bake for about 10 minutes longer or until lightly browned. Cool on a rack, then chill.

BLACK BOTTOM CHIFFON PIE

1 tbsp. cornstarch	1 tsp. vanilla
1 c. sugar	1 baked pie shell
4 eggs, separated	1 tbsp. unflavored gelatin
2 c. scalded milk	1/4 c. cold water
3/4 pkg. chocolate pieces	

Combine the cornstarch and 1/2 cup sugar. Beat the egg yolks thoroughly, then add the scalded milk gradually. Stir into the sugar mixture and cook in a double boiler, stirring until the mixture coats a spoon. Combine the chocolate and 1 cup custard mixture and stir until chocolate is melted. Remove from the heat and add the vanilla. Pour into the pie shell. Soften the gelatin in cold water, then add to remaining hot mixture and cool. Beat the egg whites and add remaining sugar gradually, beating until stiff peaks form. Fold into the gelatin mixture and pour over the chocolate layer. Chill until set. Garnish with additional chocolate pieces, if desired.

Mrs. Delbert Copley, Louisa, Kentucky

CHIFFON CREAM PIE

1 1/4 c. chocolate wafer crumbs	1/2 c. sugar
1/2 c. melted margarine	1/4 tsp. salt
1 env. unflavored gelatin	1 tsp. vanilla
1/4 c. cold water	1 c. scalded milk
3 eggs, separated	1 c. heavy cream, whipped

Combine the crumbs and margarine and press firmly over bottom and side of a 9-inch pie plate. Chill. Sprinkle the gelatin on the cold water. Beat the egg yolks, then add the sugar, salt and vanilla and add to the hot milk, stirring constantly. Cook and stir over low heat until mixture coats the spoon. Add the gelatin to the hot mixture and stir until dissolved. Chill until syrupy. Fold in beaten egg whites and whipped cream. Pour into prepared pie crust. Garnish with coarsely grated semisweet chocolate. Chill until firm before serving.

Mrs. Charles W. Lindsey, Springdale, Arkansas

COOL LIME CHIFFON PIE

4 eggs, separated	1 tbsp. unflavored gelatin
1 c. sugar	1/4 c. cold water
1/2 c. lime juice	1 tbsp. grated lemon peel
1/2 tsp. salt	1 c. heavy cream, whipped
Blue and yellow food coloring	1 baked 10-in. pastry shell

Combine the beaten egg yolks, 1/2 cup sugar, lime juice and salt in a double boiler and cook until thick, stirring constantly. Add food coloring, stirring, to obtain a deep lime color. Soften the gelatin in 1/4 cup cold water, then add to the hot mixture and stir until the gelatin dissolves. Add the lemon peel and cool until partially set. Beat the remaining sugar into stiffly beaten egg whites and combine with whipped cream, then fold into the cooled mixture. Pour into the pastry shell and chill for several hours until firm. Serve with whipped cream topping, if desired.

Mrs. Nancy Carstairs, New Orleans, Louisiana

LIME FLUFF PIE

3 tbsp. butter, melted	1/2 tsp. salt
3/4 c. chocolate wafer crumbs	1/2 c. lime juice
Whole chocolate wafers	1 c. whipping cream, whipped
1 env. unflavored gelatin	6 drops of green food color
1/4 c. cold water	1/3 c. chopped toasted almonds
2 eggs, separated	2 tsp. grated lime peel
1 c. sugar	Sweetened whipped cream

Line an 8-inch round cake pan, crossing narrow double folded 15-inch strips of waxed paper. Place foil-covered cardboard circle in bottom. Stir the butter into the crumbs in a small bowl, then turn into cake pan and press to cover bottom. Stand the whole wafers around side, overlapping slightly and pressing into crumb base. Sprinkle the gelatin over water to soften. Beat the egg yolks in a saucepan, then add 1/2 cup sugar and salt. Add the lime juice gradually and cook over medium heat, stirring constantly, until thickened. Add the softened gelatin and stir until the gelatin is dissolved. Cool. Beat the egg whites until soft peaks form, then beat in the remaining sugar gradually, beating until stiff peaks form. Fold lime mixture slowly into beaten whites. Fold whipped cream and food color into mixture. Reserve 1 tablespoon almonds and 1 teaspoon lime peel for top. Fold in remaining almonds and peel. Turn into crust. Sprinkle with reserved almonds and peel and chill until set. Hold the opposite ends of waxed paper strips and lift pie from pan. Place on chilled serving plate. Remove the paper strips. Serve with sweetened whipped cream. 8-10 servings.

CHOCOLATE SUISSE PIE

1 6-oz. package chocolate morsels	1 tsp. vanilla
2 tbsp. sugar	1 baked 9-in. pie crust, cooled
3 tbsp. milk	1 c. heavy cream, whipped
4 eggs, separated	and sweetened

Melt the chocolate over hot water and blend in sugar and milk. Cool. Beat in the egg yolks, one at a time, and add vanilla. Fold in stiffly beaten egg whites. Pour into the pie crust and top with whipped cream. Garnish with shaved chocolate and chill thoroughly.

Mrs. Ray Fountain, Biloxi, Mississippi

CHOCOLATE CHIFFON PIE

1 env. unflavored gelatin	1/4 tsp. salt
2 sq. unsweetened chocolate	1 tsp. vanilla
3 eggs, separated	1 graham cracker crumb crust
1 c. sugar	

Soften the gelatin in 1/4 cup cold water. Place the chocolate and 1/2 cup hot water in a saucepan and stir over low heat until the chocolate is melted. Remove from heat and add the gelatin. Stir till dissolved. Beat the egg yolks with 1/2 cup sugar till light and stir in the chocolate mixture, salt and vanilla, then cool. Beat the egg whites to soft peaks, then add in remaining sugar gradually, beating to stiff peaks. Fold the chocolate mixture into the egg whites. Pour the filling into the graham cracker crust and chill until firm. Garnish with whipped cream.

Mrs. Martin Lambert, Montgomery, Alabama

CHOCOLATE PARTY PIE

1/2 c. confectioners' sugar	6 tbsp. sugar
1 stick butter, softened	1 tsp. vanilla,
2 egg yolks	1 baked pastry or crumb shell
2 sq. unsweetened chocolate, melted	Sweetened whipped cream
3 egg whites	Chopped pecans

Cream the confectioners' sugar and butter until smooth and add the egg yolks and melted chocolate. Beat the egg whites until soft peaks form, then add the sugar gradually, beating to stiff peaks. Add the vanilla and fold into chocolate mixture, then pour into baked shell. Chill until firm. Top with whipped cream and garnish with chopped pecans.

Mrs. Henry C. Nance, Nashville, Tennessee

GRASSHOPPER CHIFFON PIE

1 1/3 c. fine chocolate wafer crumbs	Sugar
	3 tbsp. melted butter

1 env. unflavored gelatin

1/8 tsp. salt

3 eggs, separated

1 c. milk

1 c. heavy cream

4 tbsp. green creme de menthe

3 tbsp. white creme de cacao

Combine the crumbs, 5 tablespoons sugar and butter and pat firmly into a greased 9-inch pie pan. Bake in 450-degree oven for 2 minutes and cool. Mix the gelatin, 1/3 cup sugar and salt thoroughly in the top of a double boiler. Beat the egg yolks, milk and cream together and add to the gelatin mixture. Cook over boiling water, stirring constantly, until the gelatin is dissolved. Remove from heat and stir in the creme de menthe and creme de cacao. Chill, stirring occasionally, until mixture mounds when dropped from a spoon. Beat the egg whites until stiff, then beat in 1/3 cup sugar. Fold the gelatin mixture into the stiffly beaten egg whites. Turn into prepared shell and garnish with shaved chocolate, if desired. Chill until firm.

Mrs. Craig Danbury, Cordell, Oklahoma

STRAWBERRY-LIME PIE

2 env. unflavored gelatin

1 6-oz. can frozen limeade
    concentrate

1/3 c. sugar

1 tsp. grated lime rind

1 c. diced fresh California
    strawberries

1 c. heavy cream, whipped

Green food coloring

1 baked 9-in. pie shell

Soften the gelatin in 1/2 cup cold water. Combine the limeade concentrate, sugar and 3/4 cup water and simmer, stirring, until the sugar dissolves. Add the gelatin and stir until dissolved. Chill until syrupy, then stir in the lime rind and strawberries. Fold in the whipped cream. Tint a pale green with food coloring. Chill until mixture mounds from spoon, then pour into the pie shell. Chill for 2 to 3 hours or until set. Garnish with sliced strawberries.

LEMON TAFFY CHIFFON PIE

1/2 c. butter, melted	1/3 c. lemon juice
2 c. flaked coconut	1/4 c. unsulphured molasses
1 env. unflavored gelatin	4 eggs, separated
1/2 c. sugar	1 tbsp. grated lemon rind
1/8 tsp. salt	1 c. heavy cream, whipped
2/3 c. water	1/4 tsp. nutmeg

Combine the melted butter and coconut, then press on bottom and side of a 9-inch pie plate. Chill until firm. Mix the gelatin, 1/4 cup sugar, salt and water in a saucepan. Beat the lemon juice, molasses and egg yolks together and add to the gelatin mixture. Cook over medium heat for 4 minutes, stirring constantly, until the gelatin is dissolved. Remove from heat and stir in the lemon rind. Chill until mixture mounds slightly when dropped from a spoon. Beat the egg whites until stiff, but not dry, then add the remaining sugar and beat until stiff peaks form. Fold in the gelatin mixture, then fold in half the whipped cream. Turn into prepared shell and chill until firm. Garnish with remaining whipped cream and sprinkle with nutmeg.

Mrs. Kathryn Thomas, Big Spring, Texas

LEMON CHIFFON PIE

1 c. sugar	1 tbsp. grated lemon rind
1 env. unflavored gelatin	1/2 tsp. cream of tartar
1/3 c. lemon juice	1 baked pie shell
4 eggs, separated	

Mix 1/2 cup sugar, gelatin, 2/3 cup water, the lemon juice and slightly beaten egg yolks in a saucepan and cook over medium heat, stirring constantly, just until the mixture comes to a boil. Stir in the lemon rind, then place the pan in cold water. Cool until the gelatin mixture mounds slightly when dropped from a spoon. Beat the egg whites with the cream of tartar until frothy. Beat in the remaining sugar gradually, until stiff and glossy, then fold into filling and pour into the baked pie shell. Pile softly in swirls. Chill for several hours or overnight. Serve with whipped cream, if desired.

Mrs. Lane McWhorter, Jackson, Mississippi

LEMON CLOUD PIE

1 env. unflavored gelatin	1 1/2 tsp. grated lemon rind
3/4 c. sugar	2 c. frozen whipped topping,
1/4 tsp. salt	thawed
1 c. water	1 baked 9-in. pie shell,
1/3 c. lemon juice	cooled
2 egg yolks, slightly beaten	

Mix the gelatin, sugar and salt in a saucepan, then add the water and lemon juice and blend in the egg yolks. Place over medium heat and cook, stirring constantly, for about 5 minutes or until gelatin is dissolved. Remove from heat and add the lemon rind. Chill until slightly thickened. Place the bowl of gelatin in larger bowl of ice and water. Whip with an electric mixer or rotary beater until about double in volume. Blend in 1 1/2 cups of the whipped topping, then pour into the pie shell. Chill for 3 to 4 hours or until firm. Garnish with the remaining whipped topping and a slice of lemon, if desired.

Photograph for this recipe on page 86.

ORANGE CREAM SURPRISE

1 c. sugar	**4 egg whites**
1/4 tsp. cream of tartar	

Preheat the oven to 275 degrees. Sift the sugar and cream of tartar together. Beat the egg whites until stiff but not dry, then add the sugar mixture slowly, beating until meringue forms stiff peaks. Spread over bottom and up side of well-greased 9-inch pie plate, making the bottom 1/4 inch thick and side 1 inch thick. Bake for about 1 hour or until lightly browned. Let cool.

Filling

1 env. unflavored gelatin	**1 6-oz. can frozen Florida**
1/2 c. cold water	**orange juice, thawed**
1/4 tsp. salt	**1/2 c. sugar**
4 eggs, separated	**1/2 c. heavy cream, whipped**

Sprinkle the gelatin on the cold water in top of a double boiler to soften. Add the salt and egg yolks and mix well. Place over boiling water and cook, stirring constantly, for about 3 minutes or until mixture thickens slightly and gelatin dissolves. Remove from heat and add the orange juice concentrate. Chill, stirring occasionally, until mixture mounds slightly when dropped from a spoon. Beat the egg whites until stiff but not dry, then add the sugar gradually and beat until very stiff. Fold in gelatin mixture, then fold in the whipped cream. Turn into prepared shell. Chill until firm. Garnish with additional whipped cream and orange sections.

ORANGE CHIFFON PIE

1 1/3 c. vanilla wafer crumbs	1 6-oz. can frozen orange juice, thawed
1/4 c. butter, melted	2 c. yogurt
2 env. unflavored gelatin	2 egg whites
Sugar	Toasted coconut

Combine the crumbs and butter, then press mixture firmly and evenly against bottom and side of pie plate, building up around rim. Chill. Combine the gelatin and 1/2 cup sugar in a 1-quart saucepan and add 1 cup water. Cook over low heat, stirring occasionally, until gelatin is dissolved. Add the orange juice to the yogurt gradually in a bowl, then stir in the gelatin mixture. Chill until partially set. Beat the egg whites until frothy, then add 2 tablespoons sugar gradually and beat until stiff. Fold into the orange mixture. Chill until mixture mounds when dropped from spoon, then turn into the crust. Chill until firm. Garnish with toasted coconut.

Photograph for this recipe on page 2.

TANGY ORANGE CHIFFON PIE

16 graham crackers	1/2 c. butter
1 tbsp. flour	1 tsp. cinnamon
1/2 c. crushed pecans	1/3 tsp. salt
1/4 c. sugar	

Roll the graham crackers into very fine crumbs, then add remaining ingredients. Blend well and press into pie pan to form a lining. Bake at 375 degrees for 10 minutes.

Filling

1 tbsp. unflavored gelatin	1 tsp. orange rind
4 eggs, separated	Pinch of salt
1 c. sugar	1 baked pie shell
1 tbsp. lemon juice	Whipped cream
1/2 c. orange juice	

Soften the gelatin in 1/4 cup cold water. Mix the egg yolks, 1/2 cup sugar, lemon juice, orange juice and rind and salt in a saucepan. Cook over hot water, stirring constantly, until consistency of custard, then add the softened gelatin and mix thoroughly. Beat the egg whites until soft peaks form and add remaining sugar, beating until stiff peaks form. Fold the egg whites into the gelatin mixture, then pour into the pie shell. Chill until set. Spread with a thin layer of whipped cream and decorate with orange slices, if desired.

Mrs. Frank Love, Miami, Florida

CANTALOUPE BAVARIAN PIE

4 eggs, separated	1 tbsp. lemon juice
1 c. sugar	1 tbsp. grated lemon peel
1/2 tsp. salt	1/2 c. orange juice

1 pkg. orange gelatin	1 10-in. baked pie shell
1/4 tsp. cream of tartar	1 c. whipping cream, whipped
1 1/2 c. diced cantaloupe, drained	

Beat the egg yolks slightly in the top of a double boiler, then add 1/2 cup sugar, salt, lemon juice and grated peel. Cook, stirring frequently, until the mixture coats the spoon, then remove from heat. Bring the orange juice to a boil and pour over the gelatin. Stir until dissolved, then blend the egg mixture and gelatin mixture together and cool. Beat the egg whites with the cream of tartar until stiff, then add remaining sugar gradually, beating until whites hold stiff glossy peaks. Fold in the gelatin mixture, then add the cantaloupe, folding in carefully. Pile into the pie shell and top with swirls of whipped cream. Chill for at least 4 hours.

De Rette LaRue, Tucson, Arizona

RAJAH PIE

4 tbsp. sesame seed	Sugar
1 recipe 1-crust pie pastry	1/4 tsp. salt
1 env. unflavored gelatin	1 c. chopped dates
1/4 c. cold water	1 tsp. vanilla
2 eggs, separated	3/4 c. whipped cream
1 c. milk	Nutmeg to taste

Toast the sesame seed at 450 degrees for 2 minutes and add to the pastry dough. Roll out and fit in a 9-inch pie pan. Bake at 425 degrees for 7 to 10 minutes or until brown. Soften gelatin in cold water and set aside. Beat the egg yolks, milk, 1/4 cup sugar and salt in the top of a double boiler and cook until the mixture coats a spoon. Add the gelatin and stir until gelatin is dissolved, then chill until partially set. Stir in the dates and vanilla, then the whipped cream. Fold in stiffly beaten egg whites and remaining sugar. Pour into the pie shell and sprinkle nutmeg on top. Chill until firm.

Mrs. Helen Reed, San Antonio, Texas

CRANBERRY CHIFFON PIE

2 c. cranberries	2 egg whites
Sugar	1 c. heavy cream, whipped
1/8 tsp. salt	1 baked 9-in. pie shell
1 env. unflavored gelatin	

Cook the cranberries and 1/2 cup water in a saucepan over low heat until the skins pop. Add 1 cup sugar and the salt and cook until melted. Mash the cranberries. Sprinkle the gelatin over 1/4 cup water to soften. Add to the cranberry mixture and stir over low heat until the gelatin is dissolved. Remove from heat. Chill and stir occasionally until the mixture mounds when dropped from a spoon. Beat the egg whites until stiff, then add 3 tablespoons sugar gradually. Fold the gelatin mixture into the egg whites, then fold in the whipped cream and pour into the pie shell. Chill until firm.

Mrs. George Armstrong, Nashville, Tennessee

MINCEMEAT CHIFFON PIE

1 env. unflavored gelatin	1/8 tsp. salt
1 1/2 c. mincemeat	1 c. heavy cream, whipped
3 egg whites	1 baked pie shell
1/3 c. sugar	

Sprinkle the gelatin on 1/2 cup water to soften. Place over low heat, stirring constantly, until the gelatin is dissolved. Remove from the heat and stir in the mincemeat. Chill until mixture mounds when dropped from a spoon. Beat the egg whites until stiff, then beat in the sugar and salt. Fold the gelatin mixture into the egg whites, then fold in the whipped cream. Turn into the pie shell and chill.

Mrs. Juanita Webster, Macon, Georgia

GUAVA CHIFFON PIE

1 env. gelatin	1 tbsp. lemon juice
4 eggs, separated	1/4 c. guava jam
3/4 c. sugar	1/2 tsp. salt
1/2 c. guava juice	1 baked pie shell

Soften the gelatin in 1/4 cup cold water. Beat the egg yolks well and combine with 1/2 cup sugar, juices, jam and salt in a saucepan and cook until thick. Add the gelatin and stir until dissolved. Set aside to cool. Beat the egg whites until soft peaks form, then add the remaining sugar and beat until stiff. Combine the guava mixture and egg whites and place in the pie shell. Chill for at least 2 hours before serving. Serve with whipped cream, if desired.

Mrs. Gilbert Jackson, Yuma, Arizona

STRAWBERRY CHIFFON PIE

1 pkg. strawberry gelatin	1 lge. can evaporated milk
1 c. boiling water	1 pkg. frozen strawberries,
3/4 c. sugar	thawed
Juice of 1/2 lge. lemon	2 baked pie shells

Dissolve the gelatin in the water and add the sugar and lemon juice. Cool. Chill the milk in an ice tray until crystals form around edges of tray, then whip. Fold the gelatin mixture into the whipped milk, then add the strawberries and pour into the prepared pie shells. Chill until firm.

Mrs. Raby Miller, Cisco, Texas

FROZEN STRAWBERRY PIE

1 10-oz. package frozen	1 1/2 tsp. salt
strawberries	1/2 c. whipping cream
1 c. sugar	1 tsp. vanilla
2 egg whites	1 baked 10-in. pie shell
1 tbsp. lemon juice	

Thaw the strawberries at room temperature and place in a large mixing bowl. Add the sugar, egg whites, lemon juice and salt and beat at medium speed for 15 minutes or until stiff. Whip the cream, then add the vanilla and fold into the strawberry mixture. Pile lightly into the pie shell. Freeze for several hours or overnight.

Mrs. Sarah Bell, Atlanta, Georgia

STRAWBERRY-COFFEE CHEESE PIE

1 env. unflavored gelatin	Dash of salt
4 tsp. instant coffee powder	1 1/2 tsp. vanilla
1 c. water	1 c. heavy cream, whipped
1 8-oz. package cream cheese, softened	1 pt. fresh California strawberries
1/2 c. sugar	1 9-in. crumb pie shell

Sprinkle the gelatin and coffee powder over the water in a small saucepan, then heat, stirring until gelatin is dissolved. Combine the cream cheese, sugar, salt and vanilla in bowl and beat until fluffy, then stir in the gelatin mixture gradually. Chill until mixture is thick enough to mound slightly when dropped from spoon. Fold in the whipped cream. Reserve 8 to 10 strawberries for garnish, then cut the remaining in half. Pour half the coffee filling into the pie shell and top with the halved strawberries. Cover with the remaining coffee filling. Chill for about 3 hours or until firm. Split the reserved strawberries and arrange around edge of pie.

SUN-BLUSHED PEACH CHIFFON PIE

1 env. unflavored gelatin	1/2 c. sugar
1/4 c. cold water	1/4 tsp. salt
2 lb. fresh peaches	2 tsp. fresh lemon juice
3 eggs, separated	1 baked 9-in. pastry shell

Soften gelatin in cold water. Peel and pit the peaches. Puree the peaches in a food mill or blend in electric blender. Beat the egg yolks slightly in a medium-sized saucepan, then blend in 1/4 cup sugar and salt. Stir in the peach puree and cook over low heat, stirring constantly, until mixture just reaches the boiling point. Remove from heat. Mix in the gelatin and lemon juice and stir until the gelatin is dissolved. Chill until mixture mounds when dropped from a spoon. Beat the egg whites until stiff, then beat in the remaining sugar gradually. Fold the egg white mixture into the peach mixture, then turn into the pastry shell. Chill for about 3 hours or until firm. Garnish with whipped cream and fresh peach slices.

FRESH PEACH ANGEL PIE

1 env. unflavored gelatin	1/4 tsp. salt
1/4 c. cold water	3/4 c. milk
1 c. crushed fresh peaches	1 tsp. vanilla
2 tsp. fresh lemon juice	1 c. heavy cream, whipped
Sugar	1 baked 9-in. meringue shell
3 egg yolks	

Soften the gelatin in water and set aside. Combine the peaches, lemon juice and 1/4 cup sugar and set aside. Beat the egg yolks slightly and mix with the salt, 1/2 cup sugar and milk. Cook over hot water until milk mixture coats a spoon. Remove from heat and stir in the softened gelatin until dissolved. Chill until consistency of unbeaten egg whites then fold in vanilla, 3/4 cup whipped cream and the peaches. Turn into the prepared shell. Chill until firm. Spread with remaining cream and garnish with sliced peaches before serving.

Mrs. Richard V. Lindsey, Jr., Hockessin, Delaware

PEACHY DANDY PIE

2 egg whites	1 12-oz. package frozen
1/3 c. light corn syrup	sliced peaches
1 c. boiling water	1 tbsp. lemon juice
1 3-oz. package lemon	1 9-in. graham cracker crust
gelatin	

Beat the egg whites until foamy, then beat in the syrup gradually. Beat until stiff peaks form and set aside. Pour the water over the gelatin in a large mixing bowl and stir until completely dissolved. Add the peaches and lemon juice and stir until peaches are thawed. Fold in the egg whites. Chill until mixture thickens slightly, stirring occasionally. Fold mixture to distribute peaches and pour into graham cracker crust. Chill until set.

Mrs. Judy C. White, Oxford, North Carolina

GEORGIA CHIFFON PIE

4 eggs, spearated	1 env. unflavored gelatin
3/4 c. sugar	1/4 c. cold water
1/2 c. milk	1 c. heavy cream
1/4 c. lemon juice	1 Crumb Crust
1/2 tsp. salt	2 c. sweetened sliced peaches

Mix the egg yolks, 1/4 cup sugar, milk, lemon juice and salt together and cook over hot water until thickened, stirring constantly. Soften gelatin in cold water, then dissolve in the hot egg mixture and cool. Beat the egg whites until foamy and beat in remaining sugar, until soft peaks form. Beat the cream until stiff. Fold the egg yolk mixture into egg whites, then fold in half the cream. Line the Crumb Crust with the peach slices. Pour the filling over the fruit. Decorate top with remaining whipped cream and additional peach slices and chill.

Crumb Crust

1/4 c. sugar	1 2/3 c. gingersnap crumbs
1/4 c. softened butter	

Add the sugar and softened butter to the crumbs and blend well, then line a 9-inch pie pan. Bake for 8 minutes at 375 degrees.

Mrs. Mae Edison, Memphis, Tennessee

PEANUT BRITTLE PIE

2/3 c. brown sugar	1 tsp. vanilla
1 tbsp. unflavored gelatin	2 tbsp. sugar
Dash of salt	1/2 c. crushed peanut brittle
1 3/4 c. milk	1/2 c. whipping cream,
2 eggs, separated	whipped
2 tbsp. butter	1 baked 9-in. pastry shell

Combine the brown sugar, gelatin and salt, then stir in the milk and slightly beaten egg yolks. Cook, stirring constantly, over medium heat until gelatin dissolves and mixture thickens slightly. Add the butter and vanilla and cool until partially set. Beat the egg whites to soft peaks, then add the sugar, beating to stiff peaks. Fold into gelatin mixture. Fold in peanut brittle and whipped cream. Chill until mixture mounds and pile into cooled shell. Chill until firm.

Eileen M. Atchinson, Theodore, Alabama

ANGEL FOOD PIE

1 c. sugar	2 egg whites
1 sm. can crushed pineapple	1 tsp. vanilla
1 1/2 c. water	1 baked pastry shell
3 tbsp. cornstarch	Dessert topping
1/4 c. tapioca	

Combine the sugar, pineapple with juice, water, cornstarch and tapioca in a double boiler and cook, stirring, until thick. Set aside to cool. Beat the egg whites until stiff. Fold the pineapple mixture into egg whites and add the vanilla. Pour into prepared shell and top with dessert topping.

Mrs. Faye Hugg, Conroe, Texas

CREAMY PINEAPPLE CHIFFON PIE

1 env. unflavored gelatin	1 tbsp. lemon juice
4 eggs, separated	1/4 tsp. salt
1/2 c. sugar	1 graham cracker crust
1 1/4 c. crushed pineapple	

Soften the gelatin in 1/4 cup cold water. Combine the egg yolks, 1/4 cup sugar, pineapple, lemon juice and salt in a double boiler and cook until mixture thickens slightly. Remove from heat and add gelatin. Chill until partially set. Beat the egg whites until soft peaks form, then add remaining sugar, beating until stiff peaks form. Fold into custard and pour into the cracker crust. Chill for 2 hours. Top with whipped cream before serving, if desired.

Mrs. Albert Manning, Raleigh, North Carolina

PINEAPPLE CHIFFON PIE

1 tbsp. gelatin	4 eggs, separated
1/4 c. cold water	1/2 c. sugar

1 1/4 c. crushed pineapple
1 tbsp. lemon juice
1/4 tsp. salt
1 baked pie shell

Soak the gelatin in cold water for about 5 minutes. Beat egg yolks slightly and add 1/4 cup sugar, pineapple, lemon juice and salt. Cook over low heat until of custard consistency. Add the softened gelatin, stirring thoroughly and cool until thickened. Beat the egg whites until soft peaks form, then add remaining sugar and beat until stiff. Fold pineapple mixture into egg whites, then turn into the pie shell and chill. Spread a thin layer of whipped cream over pie, if desired.

Mrs. Betsy White, Columbia, South Carolina

PINEAPPLE-LIME PIE

1 env. unflavored gelatin
3/4 c. sugar
1 8 3/4-oz. can crushed
   pineapple
1/3 c. fresh lime juice
Green food coloring
1 1/2 c. coconut bar cookie
   crumbs
1/4 c. butter, melted
1 c. evaporated milk,
   partially frozen

Combine the gelatin and sugar in a small saucepan. Drain the pineapple, reserving the fruit, then add the liquid to the gelatin. Stir in the lime juice and enough food coloring to tint light green, then stir over low heat until sugar and gelatin are dissolved. Chill to the consistency of unbeaten egg white. Combine the crumbs and butter and press evenly over bottom and side of a 9-inch pie plate to form a crust. Chill thoroughly. Turn partially frozen evaporated milk into the chilled small bowl of the electric mixer and whip until stiff and holds a peak. Fold in the gelatin mixture lightly but thoroughly, then fold in the pineapple. Turn into the crumb crust carefully, swirling the top with a spoon. Chill for 2 to 3 hours or until firm.

RASPBERRY DELIGHT PIE

1/2 c. sugar	1 tbsp. lemon juice
2 egg whites, stiffly beaten	1/2 pt. whipping cream
2 tsp. gelatin	1 baked pie shell, cooled
1/8 tsp. salt	1 pt. fresh raspberries

Combine the sugar and 1/3 cup water in a saucepan and bring to a boil. Cook to the soft-ball stage, then pour, beating constantly, over the egg whites. Soften the gelatin in 1 1/2 tablespoons cold water and dissolve over hot water. Add to the egg white mixture and beat for 1 minute. Add the salt and lemon juice and cool. Beat the whipping cream and fold into egg white mixture. Pour into the pie shell and chill until set. Cover the center with raspberries and decorate border with additional whipped cream.

Mrs. Wesley Spivey, Frederick, Maryland

NEW ENGLAND PUMPKIN CHIFFON PIE

2 tbsp. unflavored gelatin	1/2 tsp. nutmeg
2 c. cooked pumpkin	2 tsp. cinnamon
6 eggs, separated	4 tbsp. melted butter
2 c. sugar	1 baked pie shell
2 c. milk	Sweetened whipped cream
1 tsp. salt	1 tsp. finely ground candied
1 tsp. ginger	ginger

Soften the gelatin in 1/2 cup cold water. Cook the pumpkin in a double boiler for 10 minutes. Mix the beaten egg yolks, 1 cup sugar and the milk and add to the pumpkin. Add the salt, spices and butter and cook, stirring, until the pump-

kin mixture is of custard consistency. Remove from heat and add the gelatin. Set aside to cool. Beat the egg whites until frothy, then add remaining sugar and beat until stiff peaks form. Fold the egg white mixture into the pumpkin mixture and turn into the pie shell. Cover with the whipped cream and sprinkle with the ginger.

Diane Bridges, Oklahoma City, Oklahoma

PUMPKIN CHIFFON PIE WITH OATMEAL-NUT CRUST

1 c. rolled oats	**2/3 c. minced walnuts**
3 tbsp. brown sugar	**1/3 c. butter, melted**

Preheat oven to 350 degrees. Spread the oats in a large shallow pan and bake for 10 minutes. Toss with sugar, walnuts and melted butter. Press evenly on bottom and side of a 9-inch pie pan and chill.

Filling

2 env. unflavored gelatin	**3 eggs, separated**
1/3 c. (packed) light brown	**1/2 c. milk**
sugar	**1 1-lb. can pumpkin**
1/2 tsp. salt	**1/2 c. sugar**
2 tsp. pumpkin pie spice	**1 c. heavy cream, whipped**
1 1/2 tbsp. dark molasses	**1 baked pie shell**

Combine the gelatin, brown sugar, salt and spice in a medium saucepan and mix well. Add the molasses, beaten egg yolks, milk and pumpkin, stirring until well combined. Bring to a boil, stirring constantly. Remove from heat and turn into a large bowl. Chill, covered, until firm. Beat the egg whites until foamy in a large bowl, then add the sugar, 2 tablespoonfuls at a time, beating well after each addition. Beat until stiff peaks form. Beat the pumpkin mixture until smooth with same beaters. Fold egg white mixture and whipped cream into the pumpkin mixture until just combined. Turn into the pie shell, mounding high in center. Chill for at least 2 hours or until firm.

Mrs. Linwood Mead, Oklahoma City, Oklahoma

FLUFFY PUMPKIN PIE

1/2 c. sugar	**1/2 tsp. salt**
1 env. unflavored gelatin	**2 c. frozen whipped topping,**
1 16-oz. can pumpkin	**thawed**
1 c. milk	**1 baked 9-in. pie shell,**
1 egg, slightly beaten	**cooled**
1 tsp. pumpkin pie spice	

Combine the sugar and the gelatin. Blend the pumpkin, milk, egg, spice, and salt in the top of a double boiler, then add the gelatin mixture and cook over boiling water, stirring constantly, for about 10 minutes or until the gelatin is dissolved and mixture is slightly thickened. Chill until thick. Fold the pumpkin mixture into the whipped topping, then spoon into the pie shell. Chill for at least 3 hours or until firm. Garnish with additional thawed frozen whipped topping, if desired.

RUM PIE

2 tsp. unflavored gelatin
1/2 c. cold water
2 1/3 tbsp. rum
1 1/8 c. sugar
4 egg whites, stiffly beaten

1/4 c. seedless raisins
1/4 c. chopped pecans
1 baked 10-in. pie shell
1/2 pt. heavy cream

Soften the gelatin in water in a saucepan. Add 2 tablespoons rum and 1 cup sugar and simmer for 10 minutes or until thick. Pour over egg whites slowly, beating constantly with mixer at low speed. Beat at high speed until fluffy and add raisins and pecans. Pour into pie shell and place in refrigerator until firm. Whip the heavy cream until thick, adding remaining sugar and rum gradually. Spread on pie and refrigerate for 1 hour.

Orlin R. Healy, Highlands, North Carolina

GRAPEFRUIT CHIFFON PIE

1/4 c. butter or margarine
1 c. marshmallow creme
Rum extract
1/2 c. finely shredded coconut
3 c. toasted bite-sized corn
  cereal
1 c. sugar
3 eggs, separated
1/4 tsp. salt

Grapefruit juice
2 tsp. shredded grapefruit
  peel
1 env. unflavored gelatin
1 c. quartered grapefruit
  segments
2 drops of yellow food
  coloring
Toasted coconut

Butter an 8 or 9-inch pie plate. Cook and stir the butter and marshmallow creme over hot water until syrupy. Stir in 1/8 teaspoon rum extract and coconut. Crush the cereal to measure 1 cup, then add to the coconut mixture and press in the pie plate. Mix the sugar, beaten egg yolks, salt, 1/3 cup grapefruit juice and grapefruit peel in the top of a double boiler. Cook, stirring constantly, until thickened. Soften the gelatin in 1/4 cup grapefruit juice, and add to the cooked mixture and stir until the gelatin is dissolved. Cool, then add 1/3 cup grapefruit juice, grapefruit segments and 1/2 teaspoon rum extract. Chill until partially set. Beat the egg whites until stiff and fold in the food coloring, then fold into the gelatin mixture. Pour into the prepared crust and chill. Sprinkle the top with toasted coconut before serving.

Mrs. Leo R. Kallinger, Largo, Florida

WHITE CHRISTMAS COCONUT PIE

1 tbsp. unflavored gelatin
1 c. sugar
4 tbsp. flour
1/2 tsp. salt
1 1/2 c. milk
1 tsp. vanilla

1/2 tsp. almond flavoring
1/2 c. heavy cream, whipped
3 egg whites
1 c. fresh grated coconut
1 baked pie shell

Soften the gelatin in 1/4 cup cold water. Mix 1/2 cup sugar, the flour, salt and milk in a saucepan and cook over low heat for 1 minute. Remove from heat and stir in the gelatin, then cool. Blend in the flavorings and fold in the whipped cream. Beat the egg whites until soft peaks form, then add remaining sugar gradually, beating until stiff peaks form. Fold the egg whites into the whipped cream mixture. Reserve a small amount of coconut, then stir the remaining amount into the egg white mixture and spread in prepared pie shell. Sprinkle the top with reserved coconut. Chill until 20 minutes before serving.

Mrs. J. D. Foust, Raleigh, North Carolina

COCONUT CHIFFON PIE

1 env. gelatin	1 1/2 c. flaked coconut
4 eggs, separated	1 tsp. vanilla
1/2 c. sugar	1 pt. whipping cream
1/4 tsp. salt	1 baked pie shell
1 c. milk	

Soften the gelatin in 1/4 cup cold water. Beat egg yolks until foamy, then mix in the sugar and salt. Scald the milk in a saucepan and add to the egg mixture gradually, stirring constantly. Return to the saucepan and cook until thick, stirring constantly. Add the gelatin and stir until dissolved. Cool thoroughly. Stir in 1/2 cup finely chopped coconut and vanilla. Beat the egg whites until stiff but not dry, then whip 1/2 pint cream until stiff. Fold egg whites and whipped cream into egg yolk mixture. Line bottom of pie shell with 1/2 cup flaked coconut. Pour the filling into the shell and chill thoroughly. Whip the remaining cream until stiff and spread over the pie just before serving, then sprinkle with the remaining coconut.

cream puffs, pie shells & eclairs

For extra-special occasions, wise homemakers know that an elegant cream puff brings elegance and excitement to the dessert course of any luncheon or dinner. Southern homemakers pride themselves on their pale golden, light cream puffs heaped with a variety of luscious, creamy fillings. In this section, you'll find recipes for many different cream puffs and fillings—and every one has been given the stamp of approval by a southern family.

Does someone in your family love cheese? Then celebrate his special day — a good report card, a promotion, or a birthday — with Cheese-Filled Cream Puffs. Or delight the ladies when they come to visit by offering them Tiny Coffee Cream Puffs. And few desserts please kids as well as Cream Puffs with Chocolate Sauce — they're so festive looking, you'll want to feature them at a birthday party.

This section contains more than cream puff recipes, though. There is page after page of recipes for every imaginable kind of shell. You'll find a recipe for Pecan Pastry — imagine how delightful it would be with your next custard pie. There is a Basic Egg Yolk Pastry for creating cream puff shells and other airy pastries. There's even a recipe for Quick-Toasted Coconut Crust — the perfect complement to a tart fruit pie.

Why not browse through these pages now? You're certain to find many recipes that trigger your imagination — and isn't that what creative cookery is all about!

BLUEBERRY CREAM PUFFS

1 pkg. cream puff mix   1 c. fresh blueberries
1 pkg. instant vanilla pudding mix

Prepare and bake the cream puff mix according to package directions. Prepare the pudding mix according to package directions, then fold in the blueberries. Split the cream puffs and remove the soft dough in center. Fill the puffs with the blueberry mixture. May use 2 cups whipped cream for pudding, if desired.

BUTTERSCOTCH CREAM PUFFS

1/2 c. butter   1/2 tsp. salt
1 c. boiling water   4 eggs
1 c. flour

Add the butter to the water in a saucepan, stirring until butter melts. Add the flour and salt and cook, stirring vigorously, until mixture leaves side of pan. Remove from heat and cool for 1 minute. Add the eggs, one at a time, beating after each addition. Drop by heaping teaspoonfuls, 2 inches apart, on a buttered baking sheet. Bake in a 400-degree oven for 10 minutes. Reduce temperature to 350 degrees and bake for 25 minutes longer. Do not open oven door during first 30 minutes of baking time. Cool. Split horizontally with a sharp knife.

Filling

1 c. sugar   1/8 tsp. salt
1/2 c. flour   3 c. milk, scalded

3 eggs, beaten

1 1/2 tsp. vanilla

1 c. cream, whipped

Combine the dry ingredients in the top of a double boiler, and add hot milk gradually, stirring constantly. Add the eggs and cook for 3 minutes. Cool; then add vanilla and cream. Spoon filling into cream puffs.

Butterscotch Sauce

1 c. (packed) brown sugar

1/4 c. cream

2 tbsp. white corn syrup

3 tbsp. butter

Combine all the ingredients in a saucepan and bring to a boil, stirring constantly. Reduce heat and simmer for 3 minutes. Serve over the filled cream puffs.

Mrs. Connie Taylor, Pine Bluff, Arkansas

CHEESE-FILLED CREAM PUFFS

1 c. water

1/4 lb. butter

1 c. flour

1/4 tsp. salt

4 eggs

Sugar

3 tbsp. grated orange rind

1 tbsp. grated lemon rind

2 lb. ricotta cheese

1/4 c. grated sweet chocolate

4 tsp. almond extract

Milk

18 maraschino cherries

Place the water and butter in a saucepan and bring to a boil. Add the flour and salt and stir till mixture leaves side of pan. Remove from heat and cool. Add the eggs, one at a time, beating thoroughly. Add 1 tablespoon sugar, 1 tablespoon orange rind and lemon rind and mix well. Drop by tablespoonfuls, 3 inches apart, on a greased cookie sheet. Bake for 10 minutes in a 400-degree oven. Reduce oven temperature to 350 degrees and bake for 30 minutes longer. Remove from oven and open puffs immediately to allow steam to escape. Combine the cheese, chocolate, almond extract and remaining orange rind and sweeten to taste. Blend in enough milk to make of custard consistency. Fill the puffs with the cheese mixture and top with cherries.

Karen Wakefield, Winter Haven, Florida

CREAM PUFFS FOR DIABETICS

2 tbsp. shortening

1/4 c. water

1/2 tsp. salt

1/2 c. gluten flour

2 eggs

Place the shortening in a small saucepan and add water and salt. Bring to a boil and cook until the shortening is melted. Add flour all at once. Stir constantly until smooth and mixture leaves side of saucepan and forms a ball around the spoon. Remove from heat and add the eggs, one at a time, beating well. Drop on oiled cookie sheet. Bake at 425 degrees for 40 minutes. Fill with favorite dietary pudding.

Mrs. D. S. Hurtubise, Oak Ridge, Tennessee

CHERRY CREAM PUFFS

1 stick pie crust mix	1 1-lb. 5-oz. can cherry
2/3 c. boiling water	pie filling
2 eggs	

Crumble the pie crust stick into a medium saucepan. Add the boiling water, stirring constantly. Cook and stir vigorously till pastry forms a ball and leaves side of pan. Cook for 1 minute over low heat, stirring constantly. Add the eggs, one at a time, beating with electric mixer at low speed for 1 minute after each addition. Drop about 3 tablespoons mixture onto a greased baking sheet for each cream puff. Bake in 425-degree oven for 15 minutes. Reduce temperature to 350 degrees and bake till cream puffs are dry and golden brown. Remove from baking sheet and cool. Cut off tops and remove excess webbing. Reserve 1/2 cup cherry pie filling. Fill cream puffs with remaining pie filling. Spoon reserved filling over the top. May be topped with frozen whipped topping.

Mrs. Bernice H. Rice, Prattville, Alabama

SERENA'S CREAM PUFFS

1 stick margarine	3 tbsp. cornstarch
Sifted flour	2 c. milk
2 1/4 tsp. salt	1 egg yolk
4 eggs	1/2 c. heavy cream
1/2 c. sugar	1 tsp. vanilla

Bring 1 cup water and margarine to a full boil, then add 1 cup flour and 1/4 teaspoon salt all at once. Stir until mixture forms a stiff ball and remove from heat. Beat in the eggs, one at a time, until mixture is smooth and blended. Drop by tablespoonfuls onto a greased cookie sheet. Bake at 375 degrees for 25 to 30 minutes. Turn oven off and leave the puffs in the oven to dry. Blend the sugar, cornstarch, 2 tablespoons flour and remaining salt in a saucepan and stir in the milk. Bring to a boil and reduce heat. Cook until thickened, stirring constantly. Beat the egg yolk and stir in a small amount of hot custard. Return the yolk mixture to the saucepan and cook until blended, then remove from heat. Chill, then beat in the cream and vanilla. Slit the puffs and fill with cream mixture.

Mrs. Douglas Hastings, Hyattsville, Maryland

CREAM PUFFS WITH CHOCOLATE SAUCE

1 c. boiling water	1 c. sugar
1/2 tsp. salt	1/2 c. cocoa
1/2 c. butter	1/2 c. light corn syrup
1 c. flour	1 c. milk
4 eggs	1/2 c. cream
Ice cream	1/2 tsp. vanilla

Combine the water, 1/4 teaspoon salt and butter in a saucepan and bring to a boil, stirring, until butter melts. Add the flour all at once and stir vigorously until mixture leaves side of pan. Remove from heat and cool slightly. Add the eggs, one at a time, beating vigorously after each addition. Drop by heaping tablespoonfuls onto a well-buttered baking sheet. Allow 2 inches between puffs to permit spreading. Bake at 450 degrees for 20 minutes. Reduce heat to 325 degrees and bake for 20 minutes longer. Remove from pan with a spatula. Cool and cut off bottoms of puffs. Fill the tops with ice cream and replace bottoms. Wrap in aluminum foil and freeze until ready to use. Mix the sugar, remaining salt and cocoa in a saucepan. Stir in the syrup, then add the milk and cream and cook until the sugar is dissolved. Increase the heat and boil until candy thermometer reaches 230 degrees or until a small amount forms a soft ball in cold water. Remove from heat and add vanilla. Serve warm over the ice cream-filled puffs.

Mrs. R. Anthony Tella, Tucson, Arizona

SEMISWEET CHOCOLATE MINARETS

1 4-egg cream puff recipe	1 8-oz. package cream cheese
1 c. semisweet chocolate	1/4 c. sugar
morsels	2 tsp. vanilla
6 tbsp. evaporated milk	

Spoon 8 mounds of the cream puff dough onto a baking sheet, using 2 tablespoons for each, then spoon 8 mounds of dough onto the baking sheet, using 1 teaspoon for each. Bake in a 400-degree oven for 50 minutes. Cool thoroughly. Melt the chocolate morsels in top of double boiler over hot water, then remove from the heat and cool slightly. Add the evaporated milk gradually to the cream cheese, blending until smooth. Stir in the sugar and vanilla, then fold in the chocolate. Chill until thickened. Cut the puffs in half, then spoon filling into bottom half of the large puffs and place the large puff tops on filling, hollow side up. Spoon in filling. Cut the small puffs in half and fill, then place on top. Place in the freezer and freeze until ready to serve. Sprinkle with confectioners' sugar, if desired. 8 servings.

CHOCOLATE-NUT CREAM PUFFS

1/4 c. butter	2 eggs
1/2 c. boiling water	Chocolate-Nut Filling
1/2 c. flour	Chocolate syrup
1/4 tsp. salt	

Melt the butter in boiling water in a saucepan over high heat, then reduce heat. Sift dry ingredients together and add to butter mixture all at once. Cook, stirring, until mixture leaves side of pan and remove from heat. Add the eggs, one at a time, beating well after each addition. Drop onto ungreased cookie sheet. Bake at 450 degrees for 10 minutes. Reduce temperature to 400 degrees and bake for 25 minutes longer. Cool. Cut off top of each puff and fill with Chocolate-Nut Filling. Replace tops and pour chocolate syrup over puffs.

Chocolate-Nut Filling

2 tbsp. flour	1 tbsp. butter
6 tbsp. sugar	1 tsp. vanilla
Dash of salt	1/2 c. whipping cream, whipped
3/4 c. milk	1/2 c. chopped walnuts
1 sq. chocolate	

Mix the flour, sugar and salt in top of a double boiler. Add milk and chocolate and cook over hot water, stirring constantly, until thick. Add the butter and vanilla and cool. Fold in the whipped cream and walnuts.

Mrs. Frances Grimes, Enid, Oklahoma

CREAM PUFFS FILLED WITH COFFEE CUSTARD

1 c. water	1/4 tsp. salt
1/2 c. butter	4 eggs
1 c. flour	

Place the water and butter in a saucepan and bring to a boil. Pour in the flour and salt and beat well. Remove from heat and add eggs, one at a time, beating after each addition. Drop onto a greased baking sheet. Bake at 450 degrees for 15 to 20 minutes. Reduce oven temperature to 350 degrees and bake for 15 to 20 minutes longer.

Coffee Custard

2 c. milk	1 egg, beaten
1/4 c. flour	1/4 tsp. salt
1 tbsp. cornstarch	1 1/2 tsp. instant coffee
3/4 c. sugar	1 tsp. vanilla
1 tbsp. butter, melted	

Scald the milk in the top of a double boiler. Mix the flour, cornstarch and sugar in a bowl then pour hot milk over the flour mixture, and mix well. Return to top of double boiler and cook, stirring, until mixture thickens. Cover and cook for 15 minutes. Combine the butter, egg, salt and instant coffee and stir a small amount of hot mixture into egg mixture, then stir into hot mixture. Cook and stir over low heat for 2 minutes. Cool and add vanilla. Fill cream puffs.

Mrs. Vickie Monroe, Fayetteville, North Carolina

TINY COFFEE CREAM PUFFS

1/2 c. butter	1 c. whipping cream
1 c. sifted flour	1/3 c. sugar
Dash of salt	2 tbsp. instant coffee
4 eggs	1 c. confectioners' sugar

Place the butter and 1 cup boiling water in a saucepan and bring to boiling point. Combine the flour and salt and add all at once to butter mixture. Cook, stirring constantly, until mixture forms smooth ball and leaves side of pan. Remove from heat and add eggs, one at a time, beating well after each addition. Drop by teaspoonfuls 1 inch apart on a greased baking sheet. Bake at 400 degrees for 25 minutes or until brown. Remove from baking sheet and cool. Make a slit in each puff. Whip the cream until stiff, adding sugar gradually. Combine the instant coffee with 2 tablespoons boiling water to make coffee essence. Fold half the coffee essence into whipped cream and fill puffs with whipped cream mixture. Add remaining coffee essence to confectioners' sugar and mix well. Spread over cream puffs. 3 dozen.

Mrs. Charles R. Davidson, Emporia, Virginia

CREAM PUFFS WITH FILLING

1/2 c. butter	1/4 tsp. salt
1 c. flour	4 eggs

Add the butter to 1 cup boiling water, and stir to melt butter. Add the flour and salt all at once. Cook, stirring vigorously, until mixture is smooth and forms a firm ball. Cool mixture slightly. Add eggs, one at a time and beat vigorously after each addition. Beat until mixture is smooth. Drop by tablespoonfuls onto a greased cookie sheet. Bake in 450-degree oven for 15 minutes. Reduce the temperature to 325 degrees and bake for 25 minutes longer.

Cream Filling

1/3 c. flour	2 eggs, slightly beaten
1/2 c. sugar	1 tsp. vanilla
1/2 tsp. salt	Maple sugar
2 c. milk	

Mix the flour, sugar and salt and stir in the milk gradually. Cook and stir until the boiling point is reached, then cook for 2 minutes longer. Stir a small amount of hot mixture into the eggs and return to hot mixture. Stir and bring just to a boil. Add vanilla and cool. Fill cream puffs with filling and sprinkle with maple sugar.

Mrs. Harold Bartlett, Dubberly, Louisiana

PINK CLOUD CREAM PUFFS

1 c. boiling water	4 eggs
1/2 tsp. salt	Cherry Filling
1/3 c. shortening	Confectioners' sugar
1 c. flour	

Combine water, salt and shortening and bring to a boil. Add flour, all at once, stirring vigorously. Cook for several minutes until mixture leaves side of pan. Allow to cool and beat in the eggs, one at a time. Drop from a tablespoon, about 2 inches apart, on a greased baking sheet. Bake at 400 degrees for 10 minutes. Reduce temperature to 350 degrees and bake for 25 minutes longer. Cool. Slit each puff and fill with Cherry Filling. Dust with confectioners' sugar.

Cherry Filling

1/2 c. sugar	2 egg yolks, lightly beaten
5 tbsp. flour	1/4 c. chopped drained
Dash of salt	cherries
2 c. milk	1 tsp. vanilla

Mix sugar, flour and salt in the top of a double boiler, then add milk and mix well. Add the egg yolks and blend. Place over hot water and cook until smooth and thick, stirring constantly. Cool, stirring occasionally, to prevent a skim forming on top. Add cherries and vanilla.

Mrs. David Blain, Dothan, Alabama

RICH CREME-FILLED PUFFS

1 c. water	1 c. sifted flour
1/2 c. butter	4 eggs

Combine the water and butter in a saucepan and bring to a boil. Add the flour and stir constantly until mixture leaves side of pan and forms a ball. Remove from heat and cool. Add the eggs, one at a time, beating well after each addition. Drop from a tablespoon onto an ungreased baking sheet. Bake at 400 degrees for 20 minutes. Reduce oven temperature to 350 degrees and bake for 20 minutes longer or until dry.

Creme Filling

4 tbsp. flour	1 c. sugar
2/3 c. milk	1 tsp. vanilla
1 stick margarine	Confectioners' sugar
4 tbsp. shortening	

Blend the flour and milk in a saucepan, then cook until thick and cool. Combine the margarine, shortening, sugar and vanilla and cream well. Add the cooked mixture. Fill the puffs with the filling and sprinkle tops with confectioners' sugar. Refrigerate until time to serve. 8 servings.

Roxie Jones, Core, West Virginia

CUSTARD CREAM PUFFS WITH CHOCOLATE ICING

1 c. water	1 c. sifted flour
1/2 c. butter	4 eggs

Bring the water and butter to boiling point in a saucepan, then stir in flour, stirring constantly until mixture leaves pan and forms a ball. Remove from heat and cool for about 5 minutes. Beat in eggs, one at a time and beat mixture until smooth and velvety. Drop from spoon onto ungreased baking sheet. Bake at 400 degrees for 45 to 50 minutes or until dry, then allow to cool slowly.

Custard

1/2 c. sugar	2 c. milk
1/2 tsp. salt	4 egg yolks, beaten
6 tbsp. flour	2 tsp. vanilla

Mix the sugar, salt and flour together in a saucepan, then stir in the milk. Bring to a boil over low heat, stirring constantly. Boil for 1 minute and remove from heat. Stir a small amount of the mixture into the egg yolks, then blend into the hot mixture in the saucepan. Bring to boiling point, then cool and blend in vanilla.

Thin Chocolate Sauce

1 c. sugar	2 c. boiling water
2 tbsp. cornstarch	4 tbsp. butter
2 sq. chocolate	1 tsp. vanilla

Combine the sugar, cornstarch and chocolate in a saucepan, then stir in the water. Boil for 1 minute, stirring constantly, then stir in the butter and vanilla. Keep hot until serving time. Cut off tops of puffs with a sharp knife. Scoop out any filaments of soft dough. Fill with custard and replace top. Frost with the thin chocolate icing. 8 large cream puffs.

Mrs. Grover Lombard, Decatur, Georgia

PEACHY CREAM PUFFS

1/2 c. water	1/2 c. whipping cream,
1/4 c. butter	whipped
1/2 c. flour	1 c. sliced peaches
1/4 tsp. salt	1/4 c. sugar
2 eggs	1/4 tsp. almond flavoring

Combine the water and butter in a saucepan and bring to a boil. Add the flour and salt all at once. Stir vigorously until a smooth ball forms, then remove from heat and cool slightly. Add the eggs, one at a time, beating vigorously after each addition until smooth. Drop by tablespoonfuls on a greased cookie sheet. Bake for 40 minutes at 400 degrees. Remove and cool on a rack. Cut side of each puff and fill with mixture of cream, peaches, sugar and flavoring. Garnish with additional fresh peach slices. 6 servings.

Opal Perkins, Searcy, Arkansas

STRAWBERRY CREAM PUFFS

1 10-oz. jar strawberry preserves	1 c. heavy cream, whipped
1 c. miniature marshmallows	6 cream puffs
	Confectioners' sugar

Fold the preserves and marshmallows into the whipped cream, then fill the cream puffs. Sprinkle with confectioners' sugar. 6 servings.

FRENCH CREAM ECLAIRS

1 c. water	4 lge. eggs
1/2 c. butter	French Pastry Cream
1/8 tsp. salt	Chocolate Glaze
1 c. sifted flour	

Mix the water, butter and salt in a 1 1/2-quart saucepan. Bring to a boil. Remove from heat and stir in flour all at once, using a wooden spoon. Beat vigorously. Return to heat and cook until mixture leaves side of pan and forms stiff ball. Remove from heat, then add eggs, one at a time, beating well after each addition. Pipe dough through a pastry bag fitted with 1/2-inch nozzle in 1 x 4-inch strips, 2 inches apart, on a greased baking sheet. Bake at 425 degrees for 30 to 35 minutes or until golden brown. Do not underbake. Turn off oven and pierce eclairs near the bottom with a knife to allow steam to escape. Leave the eclairs in the oven for 20 minutes. Cool. Split eclairs and fill with French Pastry Cream. Frost with Chocolate Glaze.

French Pastry Cream

1 lge. package vanilla cream pudding mix	1 egg yolk

Prepare pudding according to package directions adding the egg yolk.

Chocolate Glaze

6 1-oz. squares semisweet	3 tbsp. water
chocolate	2 1/2 tbsp. butter
1/4 c. light corn syrup	

Break the chocolate into small pieces and set aside. Place remaining ingredients in a saucepan and cook, stirring constantly, over moderate heat to boiling point. Remove from heat and stir in chocolate, stirring until chocolate melts. 12 servings.

Mrs. Jeannine Mikos, Birmingham, Alabama

ELEGANT EGGNOG ECLAIRS

1/2 c. water	1/8 tsp. salt
1/4 c. butter	2 eggs
1/2 c. sifted flour	Eggnog Filling

Combine the water and butter in a small saucepan and bring to a boil, stirring until the butter is melted. Add the flour and salt, all at once, and continue cooking, stirring constantly, until mixture forms a ball and no longer clings to side of saucepan. Remove from heat. Add the eggs, one egg at a time, beating well after each addition, then continue beating for about 5 minutes or until mixture has a silky sheen. Place about 1 tablespoon of the mixture on a greased baking sheet and spread into oblong shape, about 4 inches long. Repeat 9 times. Bake in 400-degree oven for 30 minutes. Cool thoroughly. Slice off the tops with a sharp knife and remove bits of soft dough from inside eclair shell. Fill with the Eggnog Filling. Serve with butterscotch or chocolate sauce or top with whipped cream and dribble with sauce.

Eggnog Filling

2 1/2 tbsp. cornstarch	1 tbsp. rum (opt.)
2 c. commercial eggnog	

Place the cornstarch in a small saucepan, then stir in the eggnog gradually. Cook over medium heat, stirring constantly, until mixture thickens and boils. Remove from heat. Cool, stirring occasionally, then stir in the rum. Refrigerate until thoroughly chilled.

Photograph for this recipe on page 108.

CRUMB PIE CRUST

1 c. graham cracker crumbs	2/3 stick butter
1 c. vanilla wafer crumbs	1/4 c. sugar

Blend all the ingredients and pour into a 9-inch pie plate. Distribute crumb mixture evenly, then set an 8-inch pie plate on crumbs and press firmly. Bake in 325-degree oven for 10 minutes. Cool thoroughly.

Mrs. Edward Amerson, Georgetown, Kentucky

BASIC EGG YOLK PASTRY

5 c. sifted flour
4 tsp. sugar
1/2 tsp. salt
1/2 tsp. baking powder

1 1/2 c. lard or shortening
2 egg yolks, beaten
Cold water

Combine first 4 ingredients in a bowl and cut in lard. Mix egg yolks with enough cold water to make 1 cup liquid. Pour over flour mixture and mix until smooth. Pastry for 6 crusts.

Mrs. Elah Wilkinson, Lexington, Tennessee

CHOCOLATE-CORN BREAD CRUST

1/4 c. cocoa
1/2 c. sugar
1 egg
1 c. milk

2 tbsp. oil
1 1/4 c. corn bread mix
1/3 c. melted margarine

Combine the cocoa, sugar, egg, milk, oil and corn bread mix and mix as for corn bread. Turn into a cake pan. Bake at 425 degrees until done. Cool until cold or overnight. Crumble and add the melted margarine, then press the mixture into a 9-inch pie pan. Bake for 8 to 10 minutes at 425 degrees. Add favorite chocolate pudding or lime pudding and chill.

Lillian T. Linebarger, Lewisville, Texas

COCONUT-CHOCOLATE PIE CRUST

2 sq. chocolate
2 tbsp. butter, melted
2/3 c. confectioners' sugar

2 tbsp. warm water
1 1/2 c. coconut

Melt the chocolate and add butter. Combine the sugar and water and add to the chocolate mixture. Add the coconut and press into greased pie dish. Chill. Fill with ice cream or pudding. Sprinkle with chocolate slivers, if desired.

Mrs. Eleanor Jones, Mobile, Alabama

GRAHAM CRACKER PIE CRUST

1 1/3 c. graham cracker
   crumbs
1/8 tsp. cinnamon

1/4 c. brown sugar
1/3 c. soft butter or
   margarine

Combine the crumbs, cinnamon and sugar in a mixing bowl, then blend in the butter. Press firmly against the side and bottom of a 9-inch pie plate. Bake at 375 degrees for 8 to 10 minutes or until edges brown slightly. Remove to cooling rack.

Madeline Abraham, Williamson, West Virginia

QUICK TOASTED COCONUT CRUST

2 c. moist toasted coconut   **1/4 c. melted butter**

Combine the coconut with melted butter and press evenly over bottom and side of 8 or 9-inch pie plate. Chill for about 1 hour or until firm. Fill with ice cream or fruit.

Mrs. A. B. Branch, Chickasha, Oklahoma

EGG PASTRY

3 c. sifted flour   **1 egg**
1 1/2 tsp. salt   **1 tsp. vinegar**
1 c. shortening   **1/2 c. ice water**

Sift flour and salt together, then cut in shortening until mixture resembles corn-meal. Beat egg slightly and add vinegar and water. Add egg mixture gradually to dry ingredients and mix just enough to hold dough together. Wrap in waxed paper. Roll out a portion of dough on floured surface and place in pie pan. Prick bottom and side generously with fork. Bake at 400 degrees for about 15 min-utes. Pastry will keep for about 1 week in the refrigerator or indefinitely in freezer.

Mrs. Earl Sharp, Pontotoc, Mississippi

HOLIDAY TART SHELLS

1 roll refrigerator sugar   **Desired filling**
**   or lemon sparkle cookies**

Slice cookie dough 1/8 inch thick. Place paper baking cups over back of muffin pans or custard cups. Arrange 3 cookies over each cup with edges overlapping and about 1/2 of the round extending below edge of cup bottom. Let stand at room temperature for 15 minutes, then press to seal edges and mold slightly. Bake at 375 degrees for 10 to 12 minutes. Cool and remove paper liners, then fill with desired filling.

Photograph for this recipe on page 1.

GOLDEN PASTRY SHELL

1 1/3 c. sifted flour   **1/3 c. butter-flavored oil**
1 tsp. salt   **3 tbsp. milk**

Sift the flour and salt in a mixing bowl. Pour the oil and milk into a measuring cup, but do not stir, then add to flour, stirring just until mixed. Shape into a ball and place between 2 squares of waxed paper. Roll to edges of paper. Peel off the top paper carefully. Lift the pastry and paper by top corners and invert over a 9-inch pie pan. Peel off paper and ease pastry into pan. Trim and flute edges. Prick bottom and side generously with fork. Bake at 400 degrees for 20 minutes or until browned.

Mrs. Lucile Goff, Conroe, Texas

TASTY CRUNCH CRUST

1/2 c. margarine
1/4 c. (packed) brown sugar

1 c. sifted flour
1/2 c. chopped pecans

Combine all ingredients with a pastry blender and spread in 13 x 9 1/2 x 2-inch pan. Bake at 400 degrees for 15 minutes. Crumble crust. Press against bottom and side of a 9-inch pie pan.

Mrs. Winnie Pringle, Chattanooga, Tennessee

PECAN PASTRY

1/4 c. (packed) brown sugar
1 c. sifted flour

1/2 c. chopped pecans
1/2 c. soft butter

Combine the brown sugar, flour and pecans. Add the butter and mix until crumbly. Spread the mixture in a large pan. Bake in 400-degree oven for 10 minutes, stirring frequently to prevent scorching. Remove from oven and stir well with spoon until crumbly. Reserve 3/4 cup crumb mixture, then pack remaining mixture in 8 or 9-inch pie plate. Cool. Fill with any cream filling and sprinkle remaining crumbs on top.

Mrs. Scott Sellwood, Rocky Mount, North Carolina

QUICKIE PIE CRUST

1 c. all-purpose flour
1/4 tsp. salt

1/4 c. oil
2 tbsp. milk

Combine the flour and salt, then stir in the oil and milk with a fork until well moistened. Place on waxed paper and cover with another sheet of waxed paper. Roll thin and remove top sheet. Loosen edges of pastry and turn into a pie plate. Remove waxed paper and shape pastry into plate. Pierce with a fork. Bake at 350 degrees until golden brown. 1 pie shell.

Mrs. John R. Cobb, Huntsville, Alabama

ALMOND TART SHELLS

1 c. butter
3/4 c. sugar
1 c. ground almonds

2 1/3 c. flour
1 egg

Mix all the ingredients together, then divide the dough into 36 equal portions. Shape each portion into buttered tart tins. Prick entire surface. Bake at 350 degrees for 20 minutes. Cool and fill with desired fillings. 36 servings.

Mrs. Emma Stark, Lake Charles, Louisiana

WATER WHIP PIE CRUST

3/4 c. shortening
1 tbsp. milk
1/4 c. boiling water

2 c. sifted flour
1 tsp. salt

Place the shortening in a bowl and add milk and water. Beat with a fork until smooth and thick. Add the flour and salt and stir quickly. Roll between 2 sheets of waxed paper and fit into a pie pan. Add favorite filling. Bake at 350 degrees until brown. 2 crusts.

Pat Harper, Hartwell, Georgia

AVOCADO CREAM MERINGUES

3 egg whites	1/4 tsp. cream of tartar
1/2 tsp. vanilla	1 c. sugar

Combine the egg whites, vanilla and cream of tartar and beat until soft peaks form. Add the sugar gradually, beating until stiff peaks form. Cover a large cookie pan with brown paper, then draw 8 hearts, about 3 inches in diameter on the paper. Spread the meringue on each heart, using back of spoon to shape sides higher than the middle. Bake at 275 degrees for 1 hour. Cool thoroughly.

Avocado Cream

3 egg yolks	3 tbsp. lemon juice
1 c. light cream	2 or 3 drops of green food
1/3 c. sugar	coloring
2 peeled California avocados, mashed	Raspberry or lingonberry preserves

Combine the egg yolks, cream and sugar in a saucepan, and bring to a boil over low heat, then simmer for 3 minutes, stirring constantly. Cool to lukewarm. Stir in the avocados, lemon juice and food coloring. Spoon into the cooled shells. Drizzle preserves over the top. Garnish with sour cream, if desired. 8 servings.

dumplings & fried pies

Dumplings and fried pies are individual-sized pastries filled with fruit or jam and cooked in a hot liquid. Dumplings are baked or steamed in water or juice; fried pies are, as their name implies, fried in hot fat. And both are sweet tooth pleasers treasured in southern homes.

The classic dumpling is, of course, made with apples. Treat your family to Spicy Apple Dumplings — they're the perfect finish to a stew or casserole supper. And explore the entire range of delicious dumplings with Blueberry Ring-A-Lings . . . Caramel Dumplings . . . Cranberry Dumplings . . . and Fresh Pear Dumplings. These delicious pastries will become favorite foods your family will often request.

And do serve fried pies. They are among the most traditional of southern foods — and with good reason. Anytime you want a sweet treat, feature Fried Apricot Pies . . . Fried Cherry Pies . . . or Fried Pineapple Pies. You'll soon discover why generations of southern families have prized these crisp treats.

The recipes for fried pies and dumplings awaiting you in the pages that follow are home-tested recipes — the kind that a woman carefully develops and perfects then serves when a mealtime occasion demands nothing but the best from her kitchen. Fried pies and dumplings are the finest of southern foods — and great recipes for them are waiting for you in this section.

PEACH DUMPLINGS

3/4 c. sugar
1 c. water
1 1/2 tsp. grated lemon rind
3 tbsp. currant jelly
2 tbsp. lemon juice
4 lge. peeled ripe peaches, halved

1/2 c. enriched whole bran
2 eggs, well beaten
1/4 tsp. ground nutmeg
1/3 c. biscuit mix
1 tbsp. butter or margarine
Whipped heavy cream

Combine 1/2 cup sugar and water in a medium skillet and stir over low heat until sugar is dissolved. Add the lemon rind and currant jelly. Cover and simmer for 5 minutes, then add the lemon juice. Remove a thin slice from the rounded side of peaches, then place in the skillet, hollow side down. Cover and simmer for 5 minutes. Soak the bran in the eggs for 5 to 7 minutes. Add the remaining sugar and the nutmeg to the biscuit mix, then cut in the butter until mixture resembles coarse cornmeal. Add the bran mixture and mix lightly with a fork to form a soft dough. Turn the peaches. Drop dough into hollows. Simmer gently for 10 minutes. Cover and cook for 10 minutes longer. Serve in sherbet or parfait glasses topped with whipped unsweetened cream. 8 servings.

EASY PEACH DUMPLINGS

1 1/2 c. sugar
2 c. water
3 tbsp. margarine or butter

1 3/4 tsp. cinnamon
6 peaches
1 recipe pie pastry

Combine 1 cup sugar, water, margarine and 1/4 teaspoon cinnamon in a saucepan and cook for 3 minutes. Remove from heat. Mix remaining sugar and cinnamon. Peel the peaches and cut in half. Remove seeds. Spoon the cinnamon mixture into peach cavities and place peach halves together. Roll out the pastry on a floured surface and cut into 6 squares. Place a peach on each square. Bring corners of pastry together and seal edges. Place in a baking dish and pour syrup over dumplings. Bake at 400 degrees for 40 to 45 minutes, basting occasionally with syrup.

Mrs. James Hill, Johnson City, Tennessee

APPLE JELLY DUMPLINGS

8 med. baking apples	1 recipe pie pastry
1/4 c. melted butter	Apple jelly
1/3 c. (packed) brown sugar	1 1/2 c. sugar
1 tsp. cinnamon	1 1/2 c. water

Peel and core the apples. Mix the butter, brown sugar and cinnamon. Divide the pastry into 8 parts. Roll out each part on a floured surface into a square and place 1 apple in the center of each square. Fill center of the apples with jelly and spread the brown sugar mixture on top of the apples. Wrap the apples in pastry and place in a baking pan. Bake at 350 degrees for about 30 minutes or until the apples are done. Combine the sugar and water in a saucepan and bring to a boil. Pour over the dumplings and bake for 10 minutes longer, basting the dumplings with syrup occasionally.

Mrs. W. David Holmes, Vinemont, Alabama

APPLE ROLL

1 1/2 c. flour	1 tsp. butter, softened
1/2 c. shortening	

Blend the flour and shortening in a bowl, then stir in enough water to make a stiff dough. Roll out on a floured surface into a 14 x 10-inch rectangle and spread with butter.

Filling

4 c. chopped apples	3 tbsp. flour
1 1/4 c. sugar	1/2 c. butter

Combine 3 cups apples with 1 cup sugar and spread over the pastry. Roll as for jelly roll and place in crescent shape in a greased 12 x 8-inch baking pan. Combine remaining apples, sugar and flour and place around roll. Add 2 cups water and dot with butter. Bake at 375 degrees for about 45 minutes. 12 servings.

Mrs. R. J. Bambarger, Eutaw, Alabama

OPEN-FACE APPLE DUMPLINGS

1 c. orange juice	6 med. cooking apples
1 tbsp. lemon juice	Sweetmeat Filling
1/2 c. water	Walnut-Cheese Dumpling Shells
1 c. sugar	California walnut halves
Dash of salt	Whipped cream or other
2 tbsp. butter	topping

Combine the orange juice, lemon juice, water, sugar, salt and butter in a medium-sized skillet, stirring to blend. Bring to a boil and simmer for 5 minutes. Core the apples not quite all the way through, leaving just enough apple at bottom to hold in filling. Peel, then stuff each apple with Sweetmeat Filling. Place the apples in the hot syrup, then cover and simmer for about 15 to 20 minutes or until just tender, basting frequently. Turn the apples upside down carefully, using wide spatula, the last 5 minutes to completely cook top. Lift the apples from the syrup, then drain and set upright in baked dumpling shells. Boil the syrup remaining in the pan rapidly for several minutes longer to thicken slightly. Spoon the syrup over the apples in shells or cool and serve separately as a sauce. Top each apple with a walnut half. Serve warm or cold, plain or topped with whipped cream, softened cream cheese or vanilla ice cream. 6 servings.

Sweetmeat Filling

1/4 c. finely chopped California walnuts	2 tbsp. chopped candied fruit
1/4 c. finely chopped raisins	1/4 tsp. grated orange rind

Combine all ingredients and mix well.

Walnut-Cheese Dumpling Shells

1 c. sifted all-purpose flour	1/4 c. finely chopped
1/2 tsp. salt	California walnuts
1/3 c. shortening	3 tbsp. cold milk or water
1/4 c. grated Cheddar cheese	

Combine the flour and salt in a bowl, then cut in the shortening. Blend in the cheese and walnuts. Add the milk, mixing until dough holds together. Round up into a ball and turn out on a floured board, then divide into 6 pieces. Roll each piece to a 5-inch circle and fit over the backs of lightly greased 3 x 1 1/2-inch muffin pans. Prick the surface of the dough. Bake at 450 degrees for 10 to 12 minutes or until crisp and lightly browned. Remove to wire racks to cool.

Photograph for this recipe on page 124.

APPLESAUCE ROLLS

Pastry for 1-crust pie	1 c. water
2 c. applesauce	1/4 c. margarine
1 c. sugar	

Roll out the pastry on a floured surface into a 1/4-inch thick rectangle and spread with applesauce. Roll as for jelly roll and cut into 1/2-inch slices. Place in an 8-inch square baking pan. Mix the sugar, water and margarine in a saucepan and bring to a boil. Cook for 2 minutes and pour over apple slices. Bake at 350 degrees until golden brown.

Mrs. George W. Clark, Douglasville, Georgia

ROSY APPLE DUMPLINGS

6 sm. baking apples	2 tsp. baking powder
1 c. sugar	1 tsp. salt
1 c. water	2/3 c. shortening
1/8 tsp. ground nutmeg	1/2 c. milk
1/4 c. red cinnamon candies	Chopped walnuts
2 tbsp. butter	Cinnamon to taste (opt.)
2 c. sifted flour	

Pare and core the apples. Combine the sugar, water, nutmeg and cinnamon candies in a saucepan and cook over low heat for 5 minutes or until candies are dissolved, stirring frequently. Add butter and cool slightly. Sift the flour, baking powder and salt together into a bowl, then cut in shortening until mixture resembles coarse meal. Add the milk and stir until mixed. Roll out 1/4 inch thick on a lightly floured board and cut into 6-inch squares. Place an apple in center of each square and fill centers of apples with walnuts. Sprinkle with additional sugar and cinnamon. Moisten edges of the pastry squares and fold corners over apples, pinching edges together. Place 1 inch apart in a greased shallow baking dish and pour syrup over all. Bake at 375 degrees for 35 minutes or until golden brown.

Mrs. W. R. Atkins, Tulsa, Oklahoma

SPICY APPLE DUMPLINGS

2 c. flour	Nutmeg
1 tsp. salt	Butter
2/3 c. shortening	2 c. unsweetened pineapple
1/2 c. milk	juice
6 cooking apples, pared	1/4 c. broken pecans (opt.)
Sugar	1 c. cream or evaporated
Cinnamon	milk

Sift the flour with salt into a bowl and cut in shortening. Add the milk and stir just until mixed. Place on a floured surface and roll out 1/4 inch thick. Cut into 5-inch squares. Cut the apples into eighths and remove core. Place about 6 pieces of apple in each pastry square. Sprinkle generously with sugar, cinnamon and nutmeg and dot with butter. Fold corners of pastry to center and pinch edges together. Prick with a fork and place in a large, greased baking pan. Combine 1 cup sugar, juice, 1/2 cup butter, 1 teaspoon cinnamon and 1 teaspoon nutmeg in a saucepan and bring to a boil. Cook until thickened. Add the pecans and pour over dumplings. Bake at 375 degrees until brown. Pour the cream over dumplings and bake for 5 minutes longer. Serve warm.

Toy Todd, Earlington, Kentucky

QUICK DUMPLINGS IN ORANGE SAUCE

2 tbsp. cornstarch	2 c. water
1/2 c. sugar	1 1/2 c. Florida orange juice
1/4 tsp. salt	Dumplings
1 tsp. grated Florida orange	Whipped cream
rind	Orange sections

Mix the cornstarch, sugar, salt and grated orange rind together in a saucepan, then stir in the water and orange juice gradually. Place over medium heat, stirring constantly, until mixture thickens and comes to a boil, then boil for 1 minute. Turn into an 8 x 10 x 2-inch baking dish or 1 1/2-quart casserole. Drop Dumplings by spoonfuls onto the hot sauce. Bake in 400-degree oven for 20 to 25 minutes or until dumplings are lightly browned. Serve warm garnished with whipped cream and orange sections.

Dumplings

1 1/2 c. biscuit mix	1/4 c. milk
2 tbsp. sugar	2 tbsp. melted butter
2 tsp. grated Florida orange rind	

Combine the biscuit mix, sugar and orange rind, then stir in the milk and butter and mix lightly. 6-8 servings.

BANANA DUMPLINGS WITH LEMON SAUCE

Pastry for 2-crust pie	1 1/2 c. boiling water
4 bananas, halved crosswise	Pinch of salt
Sugar	1/4 c. lemon juice
Grated lemon peel	1/2 tsp. nutmeg
1 1/2 tbsp. cornstarch	3 tbsp. butter

Divide the pastry into 8 parts and roll out each part on a floured surface into a circle. Place a banana half on each circle and sprinkle with sugar and lemon peel to taste. Fold pastry over and seal edges. Place on a cookie sheet. Prick the tops and sprinkle with sugar. Bake at 425 degrees for 45 minutes. Mix 3/4 cup sugar and cornstarch in top of a double boiler. Add the water and salt and mix well. Cook over boiling water until thick and clear, stirring frequently. Add lemon juice, nutmeg, 1/4 teaspoon grated lemon peel and butter and stir until butter is melted. Serve banana dumplings with hot lemon sauce.

Mrs. Charles Glenn, Wilmington, North Carolina

BLUEBERRY RING-A-LINGS

2 c. hot water	1/2 c. margarine
1/2 c. sugar	Biscuit dough
2 c. (packed) brown sugar	Fresh blueberries

Combine the water, sugars and margarine in a deep baking dish. Roll out the dough on a floured surface to 1/4-inch thick rectangle. Spread enough blue-berries over the dough to cover and sprinkle with additional brown sugar. Dot with additional margarine. Roll as for jelly roll and cut in 1-inch slices. Place in sugar mixture in the baking dish in a single layer. Bake at 350 degrees for about 1 hour or until brown.

Mrs. Thomas Manning, White Pine, Tennessee

CARAMEL DUMPLINGS

2 c. water	2 c. flour
2 c. (packed) brown sugar	2 tsp. baking powder
2 tbsp. butter	Milk

Combine the water, brown sugar and 1 tablespoon butter in a saucepan and cook until slightly thickened. Combine the flour and baking powder in a bowl and cut in remaining butter. Stir in enough milk to make a stiff dough and shape into small balls. Drop into boiling syrup and cook until done. 6 servings.

Geneva Garrison, Georgetown, Kentucky

CHOCOLATE DUMPLINGS

2 sq. chocolate	1 c. flour
1 1/3 c. sugar	1 1/2 tsp. baking powder
2 tbsp. butter	3 tbsp. shortening
Salt	1/2 tbsp. vanilla
1 1/3 c. water	1 egg, beaten

Mix the chocolate, 1 cup sugar, butter, 1/8 teaspoon salt and water in a large saucepan and bring to a boil. Mix 1/4 teaspoon salt, flour, baking powder and remaining sugar in a bowl and cut in the shortening. Stir in vanilla and egg and drop from teaspoon into boiling chocolate mixture. Cook until dumplings are done.

Mrs. Lucille Bentley, Shady Valley, Tennessee

CRANBERRY DUMPLINGS

2 c. fresh cranberries	1 tsp. baking powder
1 1/8 c. sugar	1/4 tsp. ground mace
1 c. water	1 lge. egg, beaten
3/4 tsp. salt	1/2 c. milk
1 c. sifted flour	Whipped cream (opt.)

Wash the cranberries and place in a saucepan. Add 1 cup sugar, water and 1/4 teaspoon salt. Cover and bring to a boil. Reduce heat and cook for 10 minutes or until cranberry skins pop. Sift flour, remaining sugar and salt, baking powder and mace together into a bowl. Combine egg and milk. Add to flour mixture and stir just until mixed. Drop by tablespoonfuls into boiling cranberry mixture and cover. Simmer for 20 minutes without removing cover. Serve with whipped cream. 6 servings.

Mrs. George Carter, Louisville, Kentucky

FRESH PEAR DUMPLINGS

1 c. water	2 c. flour
1 c. sugar	2 tsp. baking powder
1/8 tsp. cinnamon	1 tsp. salt
1/8 tsp. nutmeg	2/3 c. shortening
2 drops of red food coloring	1/2 c. milk
2 tbsp. butter	6 pears

Mix the water, sugar, cinnamon, nutmeg and food coloring in a saucepan and bring to boiling point. Add the butter. Sift the flour, baking powder and salt together into a bowl and cut in shortening. Add the milk and mix well. Roll out and cut into 6 squares. Peel and core the pears. Wrap square of pastry around each pear and place in a square baking pan. Pour syrup over dumplings. Bake at 375 degrees for about 45 minutes.

Mrs. Frank Barnes, Charleston, West Virginia

CHERRY DUMPLINGS

1/2 c. sugar	1 c. flour
2 c. cherries	1/8 tsp. salt
2 tbsp. butter	2 tsp. baking powder
2 1/2 c. water	1/2 c. milk

Combine the sugar, cherries, butter and water in a casserole and bring to a boil. Sift dry ingredients together into a bowl and stir in the milk. Drop by spoonfuls into boiling cherry mixture. Bake in 350-degree oven for 25 minutes or until brown.

Mrs. Corinne Tatum, Hyattsville, Maryland

FRIED APRICOT PIES

1 lb. dried apricots	1/2 tsp. cinnamon
1 c. sugar	10 unbaked biscuits
1/4 tsp. allspice	1/2 lb. shortening

Cook the apricots according to package directions, then mash thoroughly. Add sugar and spices and mix. Refrigerate overnight. Roll out the biscuits on a floured surface to the size of a saucer. Spread 1/2 cup apples on each biscuit. Fold over and seal edges with a fork. Fry in hot shortening until brown on both sides.

Mrs. Susie Pulley, Erin, Tennessee

APPLE PIE FRY

2 1/2 c. canned apple slices	Flour
3/4 c. (packed) light brown sugar	1/4 c. seedless raisins
1 tsp. cinnamon	2 tbsp. sugar
1/2 tsp. nutmeg	1/2 tsp. salt
1/4 tsp. allspice	2/3 c. shortening
	Confectioners' sugar

Drain the apple slices and dice. Combine the apples, brown sugar, cinnamon, nutmeg, allspice, 1 tablespoon flour and raisins. Sift 2 cups sifted flour, sugar and salt together, then cut in shortening with 2 knives or pastry blender. Add about 4 tablespoons water or enough to make a firm dough. Roll out small pieces of dough to 1/8-inch thickness, then cut into 5-inch circles. Place the apple mixture on 1/2 of each circle, then moisten edge of pastry with water and fold over. Press the edges firmly together with tines of fork. Fry in 350-degree deep fat for about 4 minutes. Drain on paper towels. Dust with confectioners' sugar. 18 pies.

FRIED CHERRY PIES

2 cans pie cherries
2 c. sugar
2 tbsp. cornstarch
1 tsp. nutmeg
1 tsp. almond flavoring

Red food coloring
4 c. flour
1 tsp. baking powder
1 c. shortening

Drain the cherries and reserve juice. Mix the sugar, cornstarch, nutmeg and reserved juice in a saucepan and cook over low heat until thick, stirring constantly. Add the cherries, almond flavoring and desired amount of food coloring and mix well. Chill. Sift the flour and baking powder together into a bowl, then cut in the shortening. Add enough cold water to make stiff dough. Roll out on a floured surface and cut into 2 1/2-inch rounds. Place 1 tablespoon filling on half of each round. Fold over and seal. Chill for at least 1 hour. Fry in deep fat at 375 degrees until golden brown, turning once.

Mrs. C. A. Mills, Oklahoma City, Oklahoma

DRIED PEACH PIES WITH SAUCE

1 lb. dried peaches
Sugar to taste
1 recipe biscuit dough
Shortening
1/4 c. butter

1 c. powdered sugar
1/2 tsp. vanilla
1/4 c. heavy cream,
   whipped

Place the peaches in a saucepan and cover with water. Soak for several hours or overnight. Cook over medium heat until peaches are tender, stirring occasionally and adding water, if needed. Mash well and stir in the sugar. Remove from heat and cool. Roll out the biscuit dough on a floured surface and cut in saucer-sized rounds. Fill half of each round with peaches. Fold over and seal edges. Prick tops with a fork. Fry in hot shortening until both sides are brown. Cream the butter in a bowl and add the powdered sugar gradually. Add the vanilla and whipped cream and mix well. Serve on warm pies.

Mrs. Dorsey Davis, Athens, Georgia

FRIED PINEAPPLE PIES

1 recipe pie pastry
1 can pineapple pie filling

Vegetable oil

Roll the pastry out thin on a floured board and cut into circles. Cover half of each circle with pie filling. Fold over and seal edges. Fry in hot oil until brown.

Amanda Hunt, Leesburg, Florida

FRIED RAISIN PIES

1 lb. raisins
1/2 orange, sliced thin
1/4 lemon, sliced thin

1/2 c. butter
1 c. sugar
Pastry, rolled thin

Place the raisins, orange and lemon in a saucepan and cover with water. Cook for 15 minutes, then remove from heat. Add the butter and sugar and mix well. Chill. Roll out the pastry on a floured surface and cut into 4-inch circles. Place 2 tablespoons raisin mixture on each circle. Fold over and press edges together. Fry in deep, hot fat until brown.

Jimmy D. Luttrell, Fort Worth, Texas

CANNOLI CICCOLATI

3 c. sifted all-purpose flour	1 egg white, slightly
1 1/2 c. sugar	beaten
1 tsp. cinnamon	3 c. ricotta or dry cottage
1/4 tsp. salt	cheese
3 tbsp. shortening	2 tsp. vanilla
2 eggs, well beaten	1/4 c. cocoa
2 tbsp. white vinegar	1 c. chopped toasted pecans
2 tbsp. cold water	Confectioners' sugar

Sift the flour, 1/4 cup sugar, cinnamon and salt together, then cut in the shortening. Stir in the eggs, then blend in the vinegar and cold water, 1 tablespoon at a time. Turn out on a lightly floured surface and knead for 5 to 8 minutes or until smooth. Wrap in waxed paper and chill for 30 minutes. Roll dough 1/8 inch thick, then cut into 6 x 4 1/2-inch ovals. Wrap loosely around 6-inch lengths of heavy-duty aluminum foil, folded in 3 thicknesses and rolled to 1-inch diameter. Seal edges by brushing with egg white and pressing together. Fry in deep 360-degree fat or vegetable oil until golden brown. Drain on paper towels. Cool slightly and remove foil. Cool completely and store in airtight container until ready to serve. Combine the cheese, vanilla, cocoa and remaining sugar and beat with mixer or blend in blender until smooth. Add 1/2 cup of the pecans, then chill. Fill fried pastry with the cheese mixture, then dip the ends in the remaining chopped pecans and dust with confectioners' sugar. Serve immediately. 16-18 cannoli.

fritters &
turnovers

Delicious fritters — tiny bits of fruit dipped in batter and fried to a crisp goodness are among the most versatile and popular of pastries. Fritters are perfect after-school fare or a quick and easy dessert for lunch or supper time. *Southern Living* homemakers enjoy preparing fritters for their families — try the recipe you'll find in this section for Apritarts, and you'll know why.

That's only one of the recipes you'll delight in discovering in this section. There are pages filled with family-approved recipes for fritters and turnovers. Like fritters, turnovers are easily prepared individual pastries that are versatile enough for snacks or desserts. A turnover filling may be anything from fruit to cheese — and often is, as these recipes illustrate.

Cheese Turnovers are not-too-sweet desserts that go nicely with a wide range of foods. Plum-Cheese Moons combine the smoothness of cheese with the tartness of plums in a taste-tingling turnover. More flavor excitement can be found in recipes for Date Turnovers . . . Fig Turnovers . . . Pecan Turnovers . . . even a typically southern Sweet Potato Foldover Pie that will delight your family.

Prepare some quick and easy fritters or turnovers soon. Feature them as a dessert, snack, or lunch box treat. You'll be delighted to see how enthusiastically your family enjoys them . . . and how they compliment you for coming up with yet another sweet tooth pleaser!

AEBLESKIVERS

2 Washington State golden Delicious apples	1/4 tsp. salt
1 1/2 c. sifted flour	2 c. buttermilk
1 tsp. baking powder	2 eggs, beaten
1/2 tsp. soda	Melted butter
	Cinnamon sugar

Peel, core and grate the apples. Sift the dry ingredients together, then add the buttermilk and eggs and beat until smooth. Heat the aebleskiver pan and place 1 teaspoon melted butter in each hole, then fill half full of batter. Cook on low heat until light brown on one side, then sprinkle top with shredded apples. Turn with a fork and brown on other side. Serve with cinnamon sugar sprinkled over the top.

DRIED APPLE FRITTERS

2 c. cooked dried apples	Sugar
Flour	

Combine the apples with enough flour to make a stiff batter, then shape into flat cakes. Fry in deep fat until golden brown on both sides. Drain and sprinkle with sugar. Serve warm.

Mrs. Thelma G. Murray, Castalia, North Carolina

APPLE-WINE FRITTERS

3 med. tart apples	1 1/2 c. sifted flour
1/2 c. white wine	3 tbsp. sugar
2 eggs, slightly beaten	2 tsp. baking powder
2/3 c. milk	1/2 tsp. salt
Vegetable oil	Confectioners' sugar

Peel and core the apples, then dice. Combine the apples with wine in a bowl. Cover and refrigerate for several hours. Mix the eggs, milk and 1 tablespoon oil in a bowl. Add the flour, sugar, baking powder and salt and stir until smooth. Drain the apples and fold into batter. Heat 1/2 inch oil in a skillet until sizzling. Drop the apple mixture by scant spoonfuls into oil and brown on both sides. Drain on paper towels and dust with confectioners' sugar. Serve warm. 14 servings.

Mrs. V. W. Moore, Richmond, Virginia

APPLE STRIPS

1 1/3 c. sifted flour	2/3 c. milk
1 tbsp. sugar	1 tbsp. salad oil
2 tsp. baking powder	3 or 4 med. apples
1/2 tsp. salt	Confectioners' sugar
2 eggs, beaten	

Sift flour, sugar, baking powder and salt together into a bowl. Mix the eggs, milk and salad oil. Stir into the flour mixture and mix until smooth. Pare and core the apples. Cut into strips and stir into batter. Drop by tablespoonfuls into deep, hot fat. Fry for about 4 minutes or until golden brown. Drain, then sprinkle with confectioners' sugar while warm. 3 dozen.

Mrs. E. M. Harper, Columbia, South Carolina

CRISPY BANANA FRITTERS

3 firm bananas	1 egg, slightly beaten
2 tbsp. orange juice	1/2 c. milk
1 tbsp. sugar	2 tbsp. melted butter
1 c. sifted flour	1/4 tsp. vanilla
1/2 tsp. baking powder	1 tsp. grated orange peel
1/4 tsp. salt	

Peel the bananas and cut in half crosswise, then lengthwise. Mix the orange juice and sugar in a bowl. Add the bananas and let stand. Sift the flour with baking powder and salt into a bowl. Mix remaining ingredients. Add to dry ingredients and stir just until moistened. Drain the bananas, then dip into batter. Fry in deep, hot fat for 2 to 3 minutes or until golden brown, then drain. Serve with whipped cream, if desired.

Mrs. Bart Wiggins, Baltimore, Maryland

LUSCIOUS PEACH FRITTERS

1 c. flour	2 eggs, well beaten
1 tsp. sugar	Peaches
1/2 tsp. salt	Powdered sugar
2/3 c. milk	

Mix the flour, sugar and salt in a bowl. Add the milk and eggs and mix well. Peel the peaches and cut in large pieces. Dip in batter. Fry in deep 375-degree fat for 3 to 5 minutes or until golden brown. Drain on absorbent paper. Sprinkle with powdered sugar.

Mrs. James H. Abell, Louisville, Kentucky

FRESH PEACH FRITTERS

1/3 c. milk	1 tsp. sugar
1 egg, beaten	1 tsp. baking powder
1 tsp. melted margarine	1/2 tsp. salt
1 c. flour	1 c. diced fresh peaches

Place the milk, egg and margarine in a mixing bowl. Mix the dry ingredients. Add to the egg mixture and stir until blended. Stir in the peaches. Drop by spoonfuls into deep, hot fat and fry for about 2 minutes or until brown. Drain on absorbent paper. 12 servings.

Mrs. Hugh Young, Perryville, Arkansas

HONEY CLUSTERS

2 c. sifted flour	Oil
1/4 tsp. salt	1 1/8 c. honey
1/2 tsp. baking powder	Blanched toasted almonds
3 eggs	to taste
1/2 tsp. vanilla	Colored sugar to taste

Mix the flour, salt and baking powder in a large bowl. Add the eggs and vanilla and blend. Turn out on a lightly floured board and knead. Divide dough into halves. Roll out each half to form a 1/4-inch thick rectangle. Cut into strips and roll with palms of hands. Cut into 1-inch pieces. Fry in oil at 365 degrees until golden brown. Place the honey in a saucepan and heat through over low heat. Stir in the fried pieces. Add almonds and sprinkle with sugar. Chill.

Mrs. L. D. Blake, Chattanooga, Tennessee

PINEAPPLE FRITTERS

1 c. sifted all-purpose flour	1/2 c. milk
1 tbsp. sugar	2 tbsp. melted shortening
1 tsp. baking powder	1 c. drained crushed
1/4 tsp. salt	pineapple
1 egg, beaten	Powdered sugar

Sift the flour, sugar, baking powder and salt together into a bowl. Combine the egg and milk and stir into flour mixture. Stir in the shortening and pineapple. Drop by spoonfuls into deep, hot fat. Fry for 3 to 5 minutes or until golden brown. Drain and sprinkle with powdered sugar.

Mrs. Henry Deese, Jefferson, South Carolina

FATTIGMANN WITH STRAWBERRIES

8 egg yolks	1/2 tsp. crushed cardamom
1/2 c. sugar	seed
1/4 c. butter, melted	3/4 tsp. grated lemon peel

1/8 tsp. salt

1 tbsp. cognac

1 egg white

1/2 c. heavy cream, whipped

4 c. sifted all-purpose flour

Solid all-vegetable shortening

Confectioners' sugar

Sweetened sliced California
    strawberries

Beat the egg yolks and sugar together in bowl until thick and yellow, then add the butter gradually. Stir in cardamom, lemon peel, salt and cognac. Beat the egg white until stiff but not dry, then fold in the egg yolk mixture. Fold in the whipped cream. Mix in enough flour gradually to make a stiff dough. Cover and chill for several hours or overnight. Roll dough out very thin, 1/6 to 1/8 inch thick, on a floured surface. Cut into diamond shapes about 4 inches long. Cut a 1-inch lengthwise slit in center of each diamond and fold 1 end through slit. Heat the shortening in a deep pan to 365 degrees. Fry Fattigmann in hot shortening until golden brown on both sides. Drain on paper towels. Sprinkle with confectioners' sugar. Serve several Fattigmann in a deep bowl topped with sweetened strawberries and cream or serve as an accompaniment with the strawberries.

Photograph for this recipe on page 136.

PERUVIAN CRULLERS

1/2 c. warm water

1 pkg. yeast

1/2 c. mashed sweet potatoes

2 eggs, beaten

1 tbsp. lemon extract

1/4 tsp. salt

1/4 tsp. mace

2 c. flour

Peanut oil

Confectioners' sugar

Place the warm water in a large warm bowl, then sprinkle the yeast over the top and stir until dissolved. Stir in the sweet potatoes, eggs, lemon extract, salt and mace. Add the flour and beat until smooth. Cover and let rise in warm place, free from draft, for about 1 hour or until doubled in bulk. Drop batter by teaspoonfuls into deep 375-degree peanut oil. Fry for about 4 minutes or until browned on both sides. Drain on paper towels. Sprinkle with confectioners' sugar and serve with syrup or jelly, if desired. 3 dozen.

APPLE AND CHEESE ROUNDS

2 c. sifted flour	1/3 c. milk
2 c. shredded Cheddar cheese	1 c. apple pie filling
1/2 tsp. salt	1/4 c. seedless raisins
1/2 c. butter	

Combine the flour, cheese and salt in a mixing bowl and cut in the butter until particles are fine. Sprinkle with milk and stir until ingredients hold together. Form into a ball. Wrap and chill for 30 minutes. Roll out on a floured surface to 1/8-inch thickness and cut into rounds with floured 3-inch cutter. Place half the rounds on an ungreased cookie sheet. Cut the apples into small pieces. Add the raisins and mix. Place a rounded teaspoon apple filling mixture in center of each round. Cut a cross in remaining rounds and place over filling. Seal edges. Bake at 400 degrees for 25 minutes or until light brown.

Edna Littlefield, Wheeling, West Virginia

APPLE CHEESIES

1 1/2 c. sifted flour	1/2 c. (packed) brown sugar
1 tsp. salt	1/2 tsp. cinnamon
2/3 c. shortening	2 tbsp. melted butter
1/2 c. oats	1/4 c. raisins
1/3 c. grated sharp cheese	6 baking apples
6 to 8 tbsp. cold water	

Preheat oven to 400 degrees. Sift flour and salt together into a bowl and cut in shortening until mixture resembles coarse crumbs. Add the oats and cheese and mix lightly. Add the water, small amount at a time, mixing until dough may be formed into a ball. Roll out on a floured surface to a 21 x 14-inch rectangle and cut into 6 squares. Mix the brown sugar, cinnamon, butter and raisins. Peel and core the apples and place on dough squares. Fill centers of apples with raisin mixture. Bring corners of dough up over apples and pinch edges together to seal. Prick with a fork and place in a shallow baking pan. Bake for 40 minutes or until apples are tender.

Bernadette Portman, Big Clifty, Kentucky

APPLE DELIGHTS

1 c. shortening	2 c. flour
1 tsp. salt	6 peeled apples, cored
1 12-oz. carton cottage cheese	Cinnamon sugar
	Powdered sugar icing

Mix the first 4 ingredients in a bowl until mixture leaves the side of the bowl and forms a ball. Chill for about 30 minutes. Roll out on a floured board and cut into 6 squares. Place an apple on each square and fill cavities with cinnamon sugar. Fold dough over and seal the edges. Place on a greased baking sheet. Bake for 30 minutes at 400 degrees. Spread with powdered sugar icing.

Mrs. G. E. Tucker, Meridian, Mississippi

BLACKBERRY JAM-CHEESE TRIANGLES

1 c. butter	1 tsp. salt
1 8-oz. package cream cheese	Blackberry jam
2 c. sifted flour	Powdered sugar

Mix the butter and cream cheese in a bowl until smooth. Add the flour and salt and blend well. Chill for 1 hour. Roll out on a floured surface 1/4 inch thick and cut into 2 1/2-inch squares. Spread each square with 1 teaspoon jam to within 1/4 inch of edge. Fold over to make triangles and seal edges. Place on ungreased baking sheet. Bake at 425 degrees for 20 minutes or until golden brown. Dust with powdered sugar.

Mrs. R. V. Clarke, Florence, South Carolina

JAM POCKETS

1 c. vegetable shortening	2 c. sifted all-purpose flour
1 8-oz. package cream cheese	Apricot, raspberry, or peach jam
1/4 tsp. salt	Cream

Cream the shortening, cream cheese and salt together, then add the flour gradually, blending well. Divide the dough into thirds and chill for several hours. Roll out to 1/8-inch thickness on floured surface, then cut into circles with 2 1/2-inch biscuit cutter or cut into 3-inch squares. Spoon small amount of jam in center of each circle. Brush edges of dough with cream. Fold over half of the dough, sealing edges with fork. Brush tops with cream, then prick with a fork. Place on ungreased baking sheets. Bake in 375-degree oven for 15 minutes or until browned. Cool on rack.

APRICOT ANGELS

2 c. butter
2 8-oz. packages cream
   cheese
4 c. flour

2 c. sugar
1 qt. apricot preserves
2 eggs, beaten

Combine the butter, cream cheese and flour in a bowl and mix well. Shape into a ball and refrigerate for 24 hours. Roll out thin on a pastry cloth. Cut into 5-inch squares and sprinkle each square with sugar. Place 1 teaspoon preserves in center of each square. Moisten edges with eggs. Fold over and seal edges. Place on a cookie sheet and brush tops lightly with eggs. Bake for 15 to 20 minutes at 425 degrees. 8-10 dozen.

Mrs. R. F. Selby, Pleasant Hill, California

APRICOT SQUARES

2 c. dried apricots
2 c. water
Sugar
3 c. flour
1/2 tsp. salt
1 c. shortening

1/2 c. milk
1 pkg. dry yeast
1 egg, slightly beaten
1/2 tsp. vanilla
Confectioners' sugar

Cook the apricots in the water in a saucepan until tender, then cool. Add enough sugar to taste. Sift flour, 1 tablespoon sugar and salt together into a bowl and cut in shortening until mixture resembles coarse crumbs. Scald the milk and cool until warm. Add the yeast and stir until dissolved. Stir into the flour mixture. Add egg and vanilla and mix well. Divide into 4 parts. Roll out on a confectioners' sugar-covered surface, 1 part at a time, to 10-inch square and cut each part into four 2 1/2-inch squares. Place a heaping teaspoon of apricots in center of each square. Pinch opposite corners together and place 2 inches apart on greased cookie sheet. Let stand for 10 minutes. Bake at 375 degrees for 20 to 25 minutes. Remove from pan immediately and roll in confectioners' sugar. Cool on rack.

Eunice Smithey, Springhill, Louisiana

APRITARTS

1 3-oz. package cream cheese
1/4 lb. butter

1 c. flour
Apricot preserves

Preheat oven to 375 degrees. Mix the cream cheese and butter in a bowl. Add the flour and mix well. Roll out very thin on a floured surface and cut in 3-inch squares. Place 1/4 teaspoon apricot preserves in center of each square. Bring 4 corners together and pinch to seal. Place on a baking sheet. Bake for 20 to 25 minutes or until lightly browned.

Mrs. Robert Hammons, Ormond Beach, Florida

APRICOT-COCONUT BITES

3/4 c. shortening
Sugar
3 eggs
1/4 c. milk
4 c. flour
3 tsp. baking powder

1 tsp. vanilla
1 box dried apricots
1/4 tsp. salt
Powdered sugar
Shredded coconut

Cream the shortening and 1 cup sugar in a bowl. Add eggs and milk and mix well. Combine the flour and baking powder. Add to creamed mixture and mix. Stir in the vanilla. Combine the apricots and salt in a saucepan and add just enough water to cover. Cook over low heat until tender. Stir in enough sugar to taste. Roll out the dough on a floured surface and cut into squares. Fill each square with apricot filling. Fold over and seal edges. Place on a greased cookie sheet. Bake at 350 degrees for 25 to 30 minutes. Roll in powdered sugar and sprinkle with coconut.

Mrs. Chris Boswell, Shreveport, Louisiana

CHEESE TURNOVERS

1/2 c. butter
1 c. grated cheese
1 c. flour
1/4 tsp. salt
Dash of cayenne pepper

1 tbsp. milk
Apple jelly
1 egg white, beaten
Powdered sugar

Cream the butter in a bowl. Add the cheese and mix. Stir in the flour, salt and cayenne pepper. Add the milk and mix well. Chill. Roll out thin on a floured surface and cut with small biscuit cutter. Place 1/2 teaspoon jelly on each circle. Fold over and seal edges with a fork. Brush top with egg white and sprinkle with powdered sugar. Bake at 350 degrees for 20 to 25 minutes. 25 turnovers.

Mrs. Milton E. Jefcoat, Sunflower, Mississippi

LOVE LETTERS

3/4 c. butter
6 eggs, separated
3/4 c. flour
Pinch of salt

3/4 c. powdered sugar
3/4 c. ground walnuts
Cinnamon to taste

Cream the butter in a bowl, then stir in the egg yolks. Add the flour and salt and mix well. Cover and refrigerate overnight. Beat the egg whites in a bowl until stiff, adding sugar gradually. Fold in the walnuts. Divide the pastry into 22 parts and roll each part out on a floured surface into very thin square. Place filling in the centers. Fold into thirds, then fold ends over into thirds, making a square. Place on a baking sheet. Bake at 350 degrees for 25 minutes or until golden brown, then remove from baking sheet. Cool. Mix additional powdered sugar with cinnamon and sprinkle over pastries.

Mrs. Betty Rowe, Santa Fe, New Mexico

BLUEBERRY TURNOVERS

1 c. soft butter or margarine	2 c. fresh blueberries
Sugar	3/4 c. (packed) light brown
1/2 tsp. salt	sugar
2 eggs, separated	2 tbsp. instant tapioca
3 c. all-purpose flour	Grated rind of 1 orange
1/4 c. milk	

Mix butter, 1/2 cup sugar, salt, egg yolks, flour and milk together until well blended and a soft dough is formed, then chill for 1 hour. Roll out dough to 1/4-inch thickness and cut out 5 to 6-inch rounds. Mix the blueberries with the brown sugar, tapioca and orange rind and spoon on the rounds. Moisten edges of each round with water. Fold dough over filling and press together. Prick top with a fork and place turnovers on a greased cookie sheet. Beat the egg whites until foamy, then beat in 1/3 cup sugar gradually. Brush mixture on top of turnovers. Bake in preheated 400-degree oven for 10 to 15 minutes or until turnovers are lightly browned. 12 turnovers.

BLUEBERRY REWARDS

1 pkg. dry yeast	2 eggs, beaten
1 c. warm milk	1 sm. can evaporated milk
5 c. flour	Sugar
1 tsp. salt	Blueberry pie filling
2 c. lard	

Dissolve the yeast in the milk. Mix the flour and salt in a bowl and cut in the lard until mixture resembles cornmeal. Add the yeast mixture, eggs and milk and mix well. Refrigerate for 4 to 5 hours or overnight. Roll out, 1/4 cup at a time, on cloth covered with sugar. Add 1 tablespoon pie filling. Fold over and press edges together. Place on a greased baking sheet. Bake at 375 degrees for 25 minutes. 40 turnovers.

Mrs. William Story, Valdosta, Georgia

DATE TARTS

1 pkg. dry yeast	1/2 c. sour cream
1/4 c. warm water	1 tsp. vanilla
1 1/2 c. flour	2 egg whites
1 c. margarine, softened	1 c. sugar
1 egg yolk, beaten	1 c. chopped dates
1/2 tsp. salt	1 c. chopped nuts

Dissolve the yeast in water in a bowl. Add flour and margarine and blend. Add the egg yolk, salt, sour cream and vanilla and mix well. Cover and refrigerate overnight. Roll out very thin on a floured surface and cut into 2-inch squares. Beat the egg whites in a bowl until stiff, adding sugar gradually. Fold in the dates and nuts. Place 1 teaspoon filling on each square. Bring opposite corners to center and pinch together. Place on a baking sheet. Bake at 375 degrees for 25 minutes or until light brown. 60 tarts.

Mrs. Mae Taylor, Tucson, Arizona

INDIVIDUAL FIG FOLDOVERS

1 c. shortening	Pinch of salt
2 c. sugar	2 tbsp. baking powder
2 eggs, beaten	1 tsp. nutmeg
1 c. milk	Fig preserves
6 c. sifted flour	

Cream the shortening and sugar in a bowl. Add the eggs and milk and mix well. Sift dry ingredients together. Add to egg mixture and mix. Place a heaping tablespoon dough on a floured surface and pat into a circle. Spoon 1 tablespoon preserves on the circle. Fold over and seal edge. Repeat until all dough is used. Place on a greased baking sheet. Bake at 400 degrees for 20 minutes or until brown.

Mrs. G. A. Cuccio, Crowley, Louisiana

CHERRY-CREAM CHEESE TURNOVERS

1 8-oz. package cream cheese	Pinch of salt
1 c. butter	1 can cherry pie filling
1 tsp. vanilla	Powdered sugar
2 c. sifted flour	

Blend the cream cheese and butter in a bowl, then stir in vanilla. Add the flour and salt and mix well. Place in refrigerator for 1 hour. Roll out thin on a floured surface and cut into 2-inch squares. Place 2 cherries from cherry pie filling in center of each square. Fold over and seal edges. Place on a baking sheet. Bake at 350 degrees for about 25 minutes. Cool and dust with powdered sugar. 50 turnovers.

Mrs. S. T. White, Montgomery, Alabama

147

CHERRY-PASTRY TURNOVERS

2 c. sifted flour
1/2 lb. cottage cheese
1 c. butter

Cherry pie filling
Powdered sugar

Blend the flour, cottage cheese and butter in a bowl. Wrap in waxed paper and refrigerate overnight. Roll out thin on a floured surface and cut into 4-inch squares. Place 1 teaspoonful pie filling in center of each square. Fold over to form triangle and seal edges with a fork. Place on a baking sheet. Bake at 375 degrees for 20 minutes or until brown. Cool, then sprinkle with powdered sugar. 2 dozen.

Mrs. Clark Matthews, Winter Haven, Florida

SIMPLE PEACH TURNOVERS

1 1/2 c. flour
1/2 tsp. salt
1/2 c. shortening

1/4 c. (about) cold water
1 1/2 c. chopped peaches

Sift the flour and salt together into a bowl and cut in shortening. Add enough water to make stiff dough and mix well. Place on floured board and roll out. Cut in 5-inch squares and place peaches on squares. Fold over in triangles and seal edges. Prick several times with a fork and place on baking sheet. Bake in 400-degree oven for 25 minutes.

Mrs. Bill Cadle, Lamont, Oklahoma

PEACH GOODIES

1 pkg. pastry mix
2 No. 2 1/2 cans peach halves
6 marshmallows
1 egg yolk, beaten

2 tbsp. milk
1/2 c. currant jelly
2 tbsp. water

Prepare the pastry mix according to package directions. Roll out 1/8 inch thick on a floured surface and cut into six 6-inch squares. Drain the peaches and place a peach half on each pastry square. Place 1 marshmallow in cavity of each peach half and place a peach half over each marshmallow to form a whole peach. Moisten edges of pastry. Fold up over peaches and pinch edges together, turning back corners to resemble petals. Mix the egg yolk and milk and brush over pastry. Place on baking sheet. Bake at 425 degrees for 20 minutes or until brown. Place the currant jelly and water in a saucepan and heat until jelly is melted, stirring occasionally. Spoon over pastry.

Mrs. W. H. Moore, Sr., Whitesboro, Texas

PECAN TURNOVERS

2 c. sifted flour
1/2 tsp. salt
1 c. butter
3 eggs, separated

3 tbsp. cream
1 c. powdered sugar
1 c. chopped pecans

Sift the flour with salt into a bowl and cut in butter. Mix the egg yolks with cream. Add to flour mixture and mix well. Shape into small balls and refrigerate overnight. Roll out each ball on a floured surface into 2 1/2-inch circle. Beat the egg whites in a bowl until stiff, adding sugar gradually. Fold in pecans. Place 1 teaspoon filling in center of each circle of dough. Fold over and seal edge. Place on ungreased cookie sheet. Bake at 350 degrees for 25 minutes or until lightly browned. Cool and sprinkle with additional powdered sugar. 30 turnovers.

Mrs. John Jedlicka, Fort Lauderdale, Florida

GOULBOURN PEARS

1 3/4 c. all-purpose flour	Butter
2/3 tsp. salt	Mixed spices
2/3 c. shortening	Milk
5 to 6 tbsp. cold water	Sugar
2 15-oz. cans pear halves	

Mix the flour and salt in a bowl and cut in shortening until consistency of peas. Add just enough water to hold ingredients together, then chill. Divide into 8 parts and roll out on a floured surface into circles. Trim and brush edges with water. Drain the pears and place a pear half on each circle. Fill cavities with butter. Sprinkle liberally with mixed spices and top each pear half with another pear half to make a whole pear. Wrap in pastry and seal edges. Place on a greased baking sheet. Roll out pastry trimmings to make leaves and place on pastry on baking sheet. Brush pastries with milk and sprinkle with sugar. Bake at 375 degrees for 35 minutes. Garnish with halved glace cherries.

Mrs. James Roberts, Durham, North Carolina

PINEAPPLE PARTY ROLLOVERS

3 1/2 c. flour	2 eggs
Sugar	1 tsp. vanilla
3/4 tsp. salt	1 can crushed pineapple
1 c. shortening	2 tbsp. cornstarch
1 pkg. dry yeast	1 tbsp. butter
1/3 c. scalded milk, cooled	

Combine the flour, 2 tablespoons sugar and salt in a bowl and cut in shortening. Dissolve the yeast in warm milk and add to flour mixture. Add eggs and vanilla and mix well. Knead on a floured surface, then shape into 2 1/2-inch balls. Chill for 1 hour. Roll out each ball on the floured surface into a circle and cut each circle into 6 wedges. Combine the pineapple, 1 cup sugar, cornstarch and butter in a saucepan and cook until thick, stirring frequently. Place 1 teaspoonful on wide end of each wedge and roll as for jelly roll. Place on a greased baking sheet, point side down. Bake at 400 degrees for 20 minutes or until brown, then remove from baking sheet.

Mrs. Dot Cherry, Norfolk, Virginia

MINCEMEAT CUTOUTS

1 9-oz. package instant	1 c. mincemeat
mixing pie crust mix	Milk

Prepare the pie crust mix according to package directions, then divide in half. Roll out half of the pastry to about 1/8-inch thickness. Cut with desired shaped 2 1/2-inch cookie cutter. Place on ungreased cookie sheet. Spoon 2 teaspoons of the mincemeat onto center of each cutout. Roll out remaining pastry to 1/8-inch thickness and cut the same amount of cutouts, then cut a small design in center of each. Roll carefully over each cutout crosswise to slightly increase size. Place one on each filled cutout. Gently press edges together with tines of fork to seal in mincemeat. Prick tops with fork. Brush top of each with milk. Bake in 425-degree oven for 10 to 15 minutes or until lightly browned. Remove sheet from oven and lift cutouts onto wire rack to cool.

DELICIOUS STRAWBERRY TURNOVERS

2 3-oz. packages cream	1/8 tsp. salt
cheese	1 tbsp. cold water
1/2 c. butter or margarine	Strawberry preserves
3/4 c. sifted flour	

Soften the cream cheese in a bowl. Add the butter and mix well. Stir in the flour and salt. Add water and mix lightly until blended. Chill until firm. Roll out on a floured board to 1/4-inch thickness and cut into 3-inch circles. Place 1 tablespoon preserves in center of each circle. Fold in half and seal edges with a fork. Place on a cookie sheet. Bake in 450-degree oven for about 10 minutes. 15 turnovers.

Mrs. Peggy Lawrence, Nashville, Tennessee

EASY STRAWBERRY PASTRY FOLDOVERS

1 c. margarine or butter	1/2 tsp. vanilla
1 c. cottage cheese	Whole strawberries
2 c. unsifted flour	

Cream the margarine and cottage cheese in a bowl. Add the flour and mix well. Stir in the vanilla. Shape into 3 balls and chill for at least 1 hour. Roll out, 1 ball at time, on a floured surface and cut into 2-inch squares. Place a strawberry in center of each square and fold into triangle. Seal edges. Place on ungreased cookie sheet. Bake at 375 degrees until golden brown.

Mrs. Joseph Dusci, Wheeling, West Virginia

RASPBERRY-CHEESE HEARTS

1 c. sifted all-purpose flour	1 3-oz. package cream cheese
1/8 tsp. salt	Raspberry preserves
1/2 c. butter or margarine	1 egg, beaten

Sift the flour and salt together into a bowl. Add the butter and cream cheese and blend with a pastry blender. Shape into ball. Cover with plastic wrap and chill. Roll out 1/8 inch thick on floured board and cut with heart-shaped cookie cutter. Place a scant teaspoon of preserves in center of each heart. Brush edges of heart with egg and cover with another heart. Press edges together with fork. Place on a lightly greased cookie sheet and brush tops with egg. Bake at 400 degrees for 15 to 20 minutes or until golden brown. Cool on rack. 2 dozen.

Mrs. Roy Staton, Arlington, Texas

PLUM-CHEESE MOONS

2 c. flour	1 c. grated cheese
1 tsp. salt	Plum or crabapple jam
1 c. butter	

Mix the flour and salt in a bowl and cut in the butter. Add the cheese and mix well. Roll out on a floured surface and cut with round cookie cutter. Place spoon of jam in center of each round and fold over. Seal edges and place on cookie sheet. Bake in 375-degree oven until brown.

Mrs. B. L. Butler, Baltimore, Maryland

SWEET POTATO FOLDOVER PIES

1 1/2 c. mashed cooked sweet potatoes	1/2 tsp. vanilla
	1/4 c. chopped nuts (opt.)
1/2 c. sugar	1 pkg. refrigerator biscuits
2 tbsp. melted butter	

Mix all ingredients except biscuits. Roll biscuits out thin on a floured surface. Place a heaping tablespoon sweet potato mixture on 1 side of each biscuit. Fold biscuits over and seal the edges with a fork. Prick tops 5 times and brush with additional butter. Place on baking sheet. Bake at 400 degrees until golden brown.

Mrs. James M. Ingram, Parchman, Mississippi

tarts & tassies

A tassie is a miniature tart — and both tarts and tassies have long been favorites with families from Maryland to Texas. The crust of a tart or tassie is just a little richer and thicker than that of a pie — making it that much more delicious! And the filling may be anything from a zingy lemon cream to a crunchy nut filling. The entire range of tart and tassie flavors is an exciting one, offering the homemaker many different ways to serve these individual pastries.

Surprise your family by serving Brown Sugar Tarts. They're delightfully rich and certain to please everyone's sweet tooth! This is only one of the many home-tested recipes awaiting your discovery in this section. As you browse through the pages that follow, you'll find recipes for Cherry Pecan Crisp Tarts, a delightful blend of contrasting flavors and textures . . . Lemon Meringue Tarts, an old favorite in new dress . . . Tartlet of Pears, a tart so elegant you'll serve it with pride on those very special occasions.

And just picture how delighted your children and their tiny friends will be when you highlight the holiday season by serving Sugar Plum Tassies. What could be more appropriate for Christmas!

For compliments . . . delicious eating . . . and easy-to-prepare tidbits, you'll depend on the tart and tassie recipes in these pages.

RAISIN-BANANA CUSTARD TARTS

1 c. dark seedless raisins	2 tbsp. butter
3/4 c. sugar	1 tbsp. vanilla
4 tbsp. cornstarch	1 c. whipping cream
1/2 tsp. salt	4 sm. bananas
2 c. half and half	10 baked 3-in. tart shells
3 egg yolks, beaten	

Chop the raisins coarsely. Combine the sugar, cornstarch, salt and half and half in a saucepan and cook, stirring, over moderate heat until mixture begins to thicken. Continue cooking over low heat for about 15 minutes longer or un*il smooth and thick. Stir a small amount of the hot mixture into the eggs then s̓ back into hot mixture. Add the butter and cook for 3 or 4 minutes longer. Remove from heat and stir in the vanilla and raisins. Cool thoroughly. Beat 1/2 cup cream until stiff, then fold into the cold custard. Slice 3 bananas into the tart shells, then top with the raisin custard. Chill until ready to serve. Beat the remaining cream until stiff, then swirl through a pastry tube to decorate the tarts. Cut the remaining banana into 10 slices and garnish each tart with 1 slice.

BROWN SUGAR TARTS

1 1/2 c. sifted flour	1 tsp. vanilla
1 tsp. salt	1 tbsp. soft butter
2/3 c. shortening	1/2 c. grated coconut
3 tbsp. milk	1/2 c. diced dates
2 c. (packed) brown sugar	1/2 c. chopped walnuts
2 eggs	

Sift the flour and 3/4 teaspoon salt together, then cut in the shortening. Blend in the milk. Roll on lightly floured board, then cut in 3 1/2-inch circles. Press into muffin tins. Combine the brown sugar, eggs, remaining salt, vanilla, butter, coconut, dates and walnuts and mix well. Spoon into the pastry shells. Bake at 375 degrees for 25 minutes.

Mrs. Norma Gilmer, Charlotte, North Carolina

RASPBERRY COCKTAIL TARTS

1 1-lb. 14-oz. can fruit cocktail	1 tbsp. lemon juice
1 3-oz. package raspberry gelatin	1/2 pt. heavy cream
	1 tbsp. sugar
3/4 c. boiling water	2 drops of almond flavoring
	Baked tart shells

Drain the fruit cocktail, reserving 1 cup syrup. Dissolve the gelatin in the boiling water, then add the lemon juice and reserved syrup. Chill until thickened. Combine the cream, sugar and almond flavoring and whip until stiff. Whip the gelatin mixture until fluffy, then blend in the whipped cream. Fold in the fruit cocktail and chill until mixture mounds on a spoon. Heap lightly into tart shells and chill until set.

Mrs. Agatha Henderson, Mobile, Alabama

BUTTER TARTS

Sifted flour	1 egg
3/4 tsp. salt	1 tbsp. milk
5/8 c. shortening	1/2 tsp. vanilla
3 tbsp. water	1/4 c. butter, melted
1/2 c. (packed) brown sugar	1/2 c. chopped pecans
1/4 c. sugar	

Combine 1 1/2 cups flour and salt, then cut in the shortening with a pastry blender. Blend in the water and shape into a ball. Line 24 tart pans or muffin tins with the pastry. Combine the brown sugar, sugar and 1 1/2 teaspoons flour and mix. Add the egg, milk, vanilla and butter and beat until thoroughly blended. Fold in the pecans, then spoon into the pastry shells. Bake at 425 degrees for 15 to 20 minutes or until filling is set.

Marguerite Gibson, Fort Lauderdale, Florida

CARAMEL TARTS

2 c. (packed) brown sugar	1 tsp. vanilla
1/4 lb. butter	18 unbaked tart shells
3 eggs	

Combine the brown sugar, butter, eggs and vanilla in a bowl and beat until well blended. Spoon into the tart shells. Bake at 325 degrees until the filling is thickened and shells are browned.

Mrs. Hugh Pfaff, Tobaccoville, North Carolina

SURPRISE CHERRY TARTS

1 tbsp. tapioca	1 c. drained pitted cherries
1/4 c. sugar	1 drop of almond extract
1/8 tsp. salt	Red food coloring
1/2 c. cherry juice	1/2 c. cottage cheese
1 tsp. margarine, melted	2 tbsp. confectioners' sugar
Dash of grated orange rind	6 baked 3-in. tart shells

Combine the tapioca, sugar, salt and cherry juice in a saucepan, then cook, stirring until mixture comes to a boil. Remove from heat and stir in the margarine and orange rind. Cool to room temperature, stirring occasionally. Add the cherries, almond extract and about 3 drops of red food coloring. Combine the cottage cheese with the confectioners' sugar and place about 1 tablespoon of the cheese mixture in each tart shell. Fill tart shells with cooled cherry mixture, and garnish with any remaining cottage cheese mixture.

Mrs. Betty M. Jackson, Pikeville, North Carolina

PIQUANT CHERRY TARTS

3/4 c. sugar	2 tbsp. butter
2 tbsp. cornstarch	1 tsp. grated orange rind
1/2 tsp. salt	4 c. red tart unsweetened
3 tbsp. orange juice	cherries
1 tbsp. lemon juice	9 tart shells
1 c. unsweetened cherry juice	

Combine the sugar, cornstarch, salt and fruit juices in a saucepan and mix well. Cook, stirring constantly, for 5 minutes or until thickened and clear. Remove from heat and add the butter, orange rind and cherries. Cool. Spoon into the tart shells. Garnish with whipped cream, if desired.

Mrs. Madaline Beasley, Wilmington, Delaware

CHERRY-PECAN CRISP TARTS

2/3 c. cherry juice	1/2 c. flour
1/3 c. sugar	1/2 c. quick-cooking oats
2 tbsp. quick-cooking tapioca	1/2 c. (packed) brown sugar
1/2 tsp. almond extract	1/4 c. butter, softened
1 20-oz. package frozen	1/4 c. chopped pecans
sweet cherries	Pastry for 2-crust pie
Red food coloring	Whipped cream

Combine the cherry juice, sugar and tapioca in a saucepan and bring to a rolling boil. Add the almond extract, cherries and several drops of food coloring, then mix well and cool. Mix the flour, oats, brown sugar, butter and pecans together, then spread in a shallow pan. Bake at 350 degrees for 10 to 15 minutes. Cool and crumble until fine. Roll out the pastry dough and cut 6 circles, then place in tart pans and prick with fork. Bake at 400 degrees for 10 to 12 minutes or until golden, then cool. Spoon the cherry mixture in the tart shells. Top with whipped cream, then cover with pecan mixture. Yield: 6 tarts.

Susan Lively Tucker, Tallahassee, Florida

QUEEN VICTORIA'S CORONATION TART

1 env. unflavored gelatin	1 baked 9-in. rich pastry
1/4 c. cold water	shell
4 egg yolks, beaten	1 tbsp. cornstarch
1/2 c. sugar	1/2 c. maraschino cherry juice
1 tbsp. grated lemon rind	1 1/2 c. drained maraschino
Lemon juice	cherries
1 c. heavy cream, whipped	Wine Whipped Cream

Soften the gelatin in the cold water. Blend the egg yolks, sugar, lemon rind and 1/3 cup lemon juice together, in top of double boiler, then cook over boiling water for about 8 minutes, stirring constantly, until thickened. Add the gelatin and cook, stirring constantly, for about 3 minutes or until gelatin is dissolved. Cool until slightly thickened, then fold in the whipped cream. Turn into the pastry shell and chill until set. Blend the cornstarch with the cherry juice and cook over low heat, stirring constantly, until thickened. Stir in 1 tablespoon lemon juice and the cherries. Top cooled tart with the cherry mixture. Chill. Serve with the Wine Whipped Cream.

Wine Whipped Cream

1/2 c. sifted confectioners'	2 tbsp. California sweet or
sugar	cream sherry
1 c. heavy cream, whipped	

Fold the sugar into the whipped cream, then fold in the sherry.

HOLIDAY CHERRY-ALMOND FILLING

1 can cherry pie filling	Confectioners' sugar
2 tsp. almond extract	1 pkg. cream cheese,
1 recipe Holiday Tart	softened
Shells	

Combine the pie filling and almond extract and spoon into the tart shells. Dust a cookie sheet heavily with confectioners' sugar, then spread the cream cheese, 1/4 inch thick, over the sugar. Chill. Dip a small star-shaped cookie cutter into confectioners' sugar and cut the cream cheese. Arrange the stars over the cherry filling.

Photograph for this recipe on page 1.

GEORGIA TARTS

1/2 c. butter	3 tbsp. milk
1 c. sugar	1 c. chopped pecans
2 eggs	1 c. coconut
1 tsp. vanilla	1 recipe pie pastry

Cream the butter and sugar together, then add the eggs, vanilla and milk and mix well. Add the pecans and coconut and mix thoroughly. Roll out the pastry and cut into 4-inch circles, then place the circles in well-greased muffin tins. Fill each pastry-lined cup with filling. Bake at 300 degrees for 30 minutes or until well done.

Mrs. W. J. Fowler, Pineview, Georgia

LEMON MERINGUE TARTS

1 c. cornstarch	1 c. lemon juice
3 c. sugar	Grated rind of 4 lemons
1/4 tsp. salt	4 tbsp. butter
5 c. boiling water	20 baked tart shells
8 egg yolks, slightly beaten	

Combine the cornstarch, sugar and salt in the top of a double boiler. Add the boiling water gradually, stirring constantly. Cover and cook over hot water for 15 minutes. Stir a small amount into the egg yolks, then stir back into the hot mixture. Stir in the lemon juice and rind gradually, then add the butter. Cook for 3 minutes. Pour into the tart shells.

Meringue

8 egg whites	4 tsp. lemon juice
1 c. sugar	

Beat the egg whites until soft peaks form, then add the sugar and lemon juice gradually, beating until stiff peaks form. Pile on the hot filling and seal. Bake at 400 degrees for 8 to 10 minutes.

Mrs. Percy Jones, Piedmont, Alabama

LEMON CREAM CHIFFON TARTS

1 c. heavy cream	1/2 c. fresh lemon juice
1 1/4 c. sugar	2 tbsp. butter or
2 tbsp. cornstarch	margarine
1 env. unflavored gelatin	1 tsp. fresh grated lemon
1/4 tsp. salt	peel
1 c. water	6 baked 4-in. tart shells
3 eggs, separated	Satin Chocolate Sauce

Allow 1/3 cup cream to stand at room temperature during preparation of filling. Combine 1 cup sugar, cornstarch, gelatin and salt thoroughly in a saucepan, then blend in the water until smooth. Beat the egg yolks until light, then blend with the lemon juice into saucepan and add the butter. Bring to a boil and cook for 2 to 3 minutes stirring constantly. Remove from the heat and stir vigorously while adding the 1/3 cup cream and grated peel gradually. Transfer to cooled bowl and chill until thickened, but not set. Mixture should mound slightly when dropped from spoon. Beat the egg whites to the soft-peak stage, then add the remaining sugar, beating until stiff, but not dry. Whip the remaining cream until stiff. Fold egg whites and whipped cream together gently into chilled mixture. Spoon into tart shells and chill until firm. Drizzle Satin Chocolate Sauce over tops of tarts and serve with the remaining sauce.

Satin Chocolate Sauce

1/2 c. semisweet chocolate	1/2 c. light corn syrup
pieces	1/4 c. evaporated milk

Combine the chocolate and corn syrup in a saucepan and place over low heat, stirring until melted and smooth. Blend in the evaporated milk quickly and simmer for 1 minute. Cool.

Photograph for this recipe on cover.

TANGY LEMON TARTS

3 c. sifted flour	1/2 c. lemon juice
1 1/2 tsp. salt	2 c. sugar
1 c. shortening	1 c. butter
6 tbsp. cold water	4 eggs, well beaten
Grated rind of 2 lemons	

Combine the flour and salt in a bowl, then cut in the shortening to the consistency of cornmeal. Add the water and stir with a fork until dough clings together. Press the dough into tart pans and prick with a fork. Bake at 450 degrees for 10 to 15 minutes or until browned. Cool. Combine the lemon rind, lemon juice and sugar in top of a double boiler, then add the butter. Cook over boiling water, stirring, until butter is melted. Add the eggs slowly, stirring vigorously. Cook, stirring constantly for about 15 minutes or until mixture thickens. Place the filling in the tart shells and garnish with whipped cream.

Mrs. C. A. Ashley, Ocilla, Georgia

HOLIDAY LEMON CREAM FILLING

1 can lemon pie filling	1 c. sour cream
1 recipe Holiday Tart Shells	1/4 c. confectioners' sugar

Reserve 1/4 cup pie filling. Spoon the remaining filling into the tart shells. Combine the sour cream, confectioners' sugar and reserved pie filling and beat until smooth. Spread over the pie filling. Garnish with red and green candied cherries.

Photograph for this recipe on page 1.

HOLIDAY PEACH GLACE FILLING

2 tbsp. cornstarch	1 can peach pie filling
2 tbsp. red cinnamon candies	1 recipe Holiday Tart Shells

Combine 1 cup water, cornstarch and candies in a small saucepan. Cook, stirring constantly, until thick and clear, then cool. Spoon pie filling into the tart shells. Spread cinnamon glaze over filling. Garnish with whipped cream and cinnamon candies.

Photograph for this recipe on page 1.

BUTTERSCOTCH PEACH TARTS

6 tbsp. melted butter	2 tsp. lemon juice
3 tbsp. flour	Pinch of salt
1/4 c. corn syrup	1 recipe pie pastry
3/4 c. (packed) brown sugar	12 canned peach halves
1/2 tsp. mace	

Combine the butter and flour in a saucepan, then add the syrup, brown sugar, mace, lemon juice and salt. Cook, stirring constantly, until thick. Line 12 muffin cups with pastry dough, then place the peaches, hollow-side up, on pastry. Cover with the sauce. Cover with strips of pastry. Bake at 450 degrees for 15 minutes. Reduce the temperature to 400 degrees and bake for 15 minutes longer. 12 servings.

Mrs. Preston Herring, Orrum, North Carolina

PEACH PERFECTION TARTS

1 No. 2 1/2 can sliced peaches	1/2 tsp. almond extract
1 pkg. vanilla pudding mix	1 c. whipping cream, whipped
1 1/4 c. milk	8 baked tart shells

Drain the peaches, reserving 1/2 cup syrup. Prepare the pudding mix according to package directions, using the reserved peach syrup and milk for liquid. Chill thoroughly. Fold in the almond extract and whipped cream. Reserve several peach slices for garnish, then fold the remaining peaches into the cream mixture. Spoon into the tart shells. Garnish with the reserved peach slices just before serving.

Claude W. Dodd, Durant, Mississippi

HALF PUFF PASTE WITH COCONUT FILLING

1/4 c. sugar	1/2 c. margarine
1 1/3 c. flour	1 egg yolk

Sift the sugar and flour together, then cut in the margarine. Add the egg and blend until mixture holds together. Chill thoroughly. Press the mixture into small fluted tart pans.

Coconut Filling

3/8 c. margarine	2 eggs
3/4 c. sugar	3/4 to 1 c. flaked coconut

Cream the margarine and sugar together until smooth, then add the eggs, one at a time, beating well after each addition. Blend in the coconut, then fill the tart shells. Bake at 350 degrees until the filling is set and browned. Cool, then turn out of pans.

COCONUT-WALNUT PIES

1 recipe pie pastry	1 c. sugar
1 c. raisins	1/2 c. melted butter
1 c. chopped walnuts	2 eggs, separated
1/3 c. moist shredded coconut	

Line 12 muffin tins with the pastry. Combine the raisins, walnuts, coconut, sugar and butter and mix thoroughly. Stir in the egg yolks. Fold in the beaten egg whites, then turn into the pastry-lined muffin cups. Bake at 350 degrees for 30 minutes. Serve with whipped cream. 12 servings.

Mrs. Della Hopkins, Lexington, Kentucky

COCONUT-ORANGE TARTS

1/2 c. cake flour	2 tbsp. lemon juice
1 c. sugar	Grated rind of 1 orange
1/4 tsp. salt	1 egg white, stiffly beaten
1 c. orange juice	8 baked tart shells
2 egg yolks, slightly beaten	Meringue
1 tbsp. butter	

Combine the flour, sugar and salt, then add the orange juice gradually. Place in a double boiler and cook until thickened, stirring constantly. Stir a small amount of orange juice mixture into the egg yolks, then return to the double boiler. Cook, stirring constantly, for 4 minutes longer. Add butter, lemon juice and orange rind, then cool. Fold in the egg white. Pour the filling into the tart shells, then top with the Meringue. Bake at 425 degrees until Meringue is brown.

Meringue

2 tbsp. sugar	1 egg white, stiffly beaten
1/2 c. coconut	

Fold the sugar and coconut into egg white.

Mrs. Helen Moore, Dublin, Georgia

PINEAPPLE-LIME TARTS

1 c. pineapple juice	6 baked 4-in. tart shells
1 pkg. lime gelatin	6 pineapple slices
3/4 c. whipping cream	

Combine the pineapple juice and 3/4 cup water in a saucepan and bring to a boil. Remove from heat and add the gelatin, stirring until gelatin is dissolved. Chill until slightly thickened. Whip the cream until stiff, then fold into the gelatin. Fill the tart shells and chill until set. Top with a pineapple slice just before serving. Garnish with a maraschino cherry, if desired.

Mrs. Gladys Fletcher, Maryville, Tennessee

PEACH-RAISIN TARTS

1 1-lb. 13-oz. can peach halves
3/4 c. hot water
2 c. seedless raisins
1/2 c. sugar
2 tbsp. cornstarch
3/4 tsp. cinnamon
1/2 tsp. nutmeg

1/4 tsp. salt
2 tbsp. butter or margarine
1/4 c. orange juice
1 tsp. grated orange rind
2 eggs, slightly beaten
6 baked 4 1/2-in. tart shells

Drain the peaches and reserve 1 cup syrup. Mix the reserved syrup, water and raisins in a saucepan and bring to boiling point. Cover. Simmer for 15 minutes. Mix the sugar, cornstarch, spices and salt and stir into raisin mixture. Cook, stirring, until thick and clear. Add the butter, orange juice and grated rind and stir until butter melts. Stir into eggs. Return to saucepan and cook, stirring, for 2 minutes longer. Cool. Fill tart shells 3/4 full with raisin mixture and top with peach halves. Serve with cream, if desired. 6 servings.

Mrs. Emil Anderson, Crossville, Tennessee

PINK CLOUD TART

2 env. unflavored gelatin
2 c. cranberry juice cocktail
1/2 c. sugar
1 c. applesauce
2 tsp. lemon juice

1/2 tsp. grated lemon rind
1 4 1/2-oz. package frozen
   whipped topping, thawed
1 baked 9-in. tart shell

Sprinkle the gelatin over the cranberry juice in a saucepan, then add the sugar and let stand for 5 minutes. Stir over low heat until sugar and gelatin are dissolved. Stir in the applesauce, lemon juice and rind. Chill until mixture thickens slightly. Fold in whipped topping. Spoon mixture lightly into tart shell. Chill until firm. Serve garnished with additional whipped topping and finely diced jellied cranberry sauce or cranberry-orange relish.

RUFFLED PEAR TART

1 1/2 c. all-purpose flour	4 or 5 fresh California
3/4 tsp. salt	Bartlett pears
2 tsp. grated orange rind	2/3 c. sugar
1/2 c. shortening	2 tbsp. cornstarch
6 tbsp. orange juice	1 tbsp. butter or margarine

Mix the flour, 1/2 teaspoon salt and 1 teaspoon orange rind together, then cut in the shortening until mixture resembles coarse meal. Add 3 tablespoons of the orange juice and toss to moisten. Press 1/4 of the mixture into a ball, then cover and set aside. Press the remaining pastry into a ball and roll on floured surface into 12-inch circle. Fit into a 9-inch round layer cake pan with removable bottom, allowing the pastry to extend about 1 inch up side of pan, then flute the edge. Pare, halve and core the pears. Reserve 1 pear, then dice the remaining to make 4 cups. Combine the diced pears, sugar, cornstarch, butter and the remaining salt, orange rind and juice in a saucepan. Cook, stirring frequently, until mixture comes to a boil, then reduce heat and cook for 5 minutes. Turn into the pastry-lined pan. Slice the reserved pear and arrange over top. Roll the reserved pastry into a 14 x 2 1/4-inch strip, then cut into 3/4-inch strips. Twist strips and arrange spiral fashion over fruit, moistening the ends and pinching together to make a continuous spiral. Bake on lowest shelf of oven at 400 degrees for 35 to 40 minutes or until pastry is golden. Cool. Remove side of pan and place on serving plate. Cut into wedges and serve with whipped cream, if desired.

Photograph for this recipe on page 152.

TARTLETS OF PEARS

1 c. flour	1/2 c. milk
1/4 c. sugar	1 tbsp. cointreau
1/2 c. butter	1 c. whipped cream
1 egg yolk	Red currant jelly
1 tbsp. coffee cream	Pear slices
Dash of cinnamon	Toasted sliced almonds
1/2 pkg. instant vanilla pudding mix	

Combine the flour and sugar, then cut in the butter until crumbly. Add the egg yolk, cream and cinnamon and blend thoroughly. Chill in the refrigerator for 15 minutes. Roll dough to 1/8-inch thickness and cut into 3-inch diameter circles. Place the circles in muffin tin. Press empty cupcake paper in each tartlet to keep dough from rising. Bake at 375 degrees for 15 minutes or until browned. Remove the paper cups and cool. Combine the pudding mix, milk and cointreau and beat for 5 minutes at medium speed of mixer. Fold in the whipped cream. Spread a thin layer of jelly in each pastry shell, then pour in the filling. Place a pear slice on top and sprinkle with almonds.

Peggy Dowd Schulze, San Angelo, Texas

HOLIDAY APPLE FILLING

2 3-oz. packages cream	1 c. confectioners' sugar
cheese	1/2 c. heavy cream

1 tsp. grated orange rind
1 recipe Holiday Tart
   Shells

1 can apple pie filling
Unbaked star-shaped sugar
   cookies

Combine the cream cheese and confectioners' sugar and beat until fluffy. Beat the cream until thick, then fold the cream and orange rind into the cream cheese mixture. Spread 1 tablespoon of the mixture over bottom and side of each tart shell. Spoon apple filling over top. Bake the cookies at 375 degrees for 5 to 7 minutes or until light golden brown. Remove from oven and punch hole, the size of small candle, in center of each cookie, then cool for 2 minutes. Remove from cookie sheet and cool thoroughly. Place cookies on tarts and place small candle in each hole.

Photograph for this recipe on page 1.

BLUE CHEESE-APPLE TARTS

1 c. sifted all-purpose flour
1/4 tsp. salt
1/4 c. butter, softened
1/2 c. crumbled blue cheese
3 c. pared diced Washington
   State apples

1/4 c. raisins
Sugar
1/2 c. sour cream
1 tsp. lemon juice
1/8 tsp. cinnamon

Preheat the oven to 425 degrees. Combine the flour and salt in a mixing bowl. Cut in the butter and cheese with a pastry blender until mixture resembles coarse meal, then blend in 3 tablespoons water with a fork. Chill the dough thoroughly. Press the dough to bottoms and sides of sixteen 2 1/2-inch tart pans. Prick with fork. Bake for 10 to 12 minutes or until lightly browned. Combine the apples, raisins, 1/4 cup sugar and 2 tablespoons water in a saucepan. Bring to a boil, then reduce the heat and simmer until the apples are transparent. Spoon into the tart shells. Combine the sour cream, lemon juice, cinnamon and 1 teaspoon sugar, then mix well and place 1 teaspoon of the mixture on each tart. Return to the oven and bake for 4 or 5 minutes longer or until glaze is just set. Remove from pans and serve warm or cool.

CHEESECAKE TASSIES

1/2 c. butter, softened	1 c. flour
1 8-oz. package cream cheese	1 egg
Sugar	1/4 tsp. vanilla
1/4 tsp. cinnamon	Strawberry pie filling

Cream the butter, 1/3 of the cream cheese and 1 tablespoon sugar in a bowl. Sift the cinnamon with flour and add to creamed mixture gradually, blending well. Shape into 24 balls and chill for 2 hours. Press each ball into a 1 3/4-inch muffin cup. Cream remaining cream cheese and 1/4 cup sugar in a bowl. Add egg and vanilla and beat thoroughly. Pour into tart shells. Bake at 350 degrees for 20 minutes. Loosen in pan and cool slightly. Remove from pan carefully. Place 1 teaspoon pie filling on each tassie and chill.

Mrs. Thomas Betts, Tupelo, Mississippi

SUGARPLUM TASSIES

1 3-oz. package cream cheese, softened	1 egg
1/2 c. butter, softened	1/4 c. sugar
1 c. sifted flour	1/4 tsp. vanilla
1 can plums	1/2 c. orange juice

Preheat oven to 325 degrees. Blend cream cheese and butter in a bowl, then stir in the flour. Roll out on lightly floured board and cut with miniature cookie cutter. Press into 1 3/4-inch muffin cups. Drain the plums and cut in half. Beat egg in a bowl until frothy. Add the sugar, vanilla and orange juice and pour into lined muffin cups. Place 1 plum half, cut side down, in each cup. Bake for 30 minutes. Remove from cups carefully.

Mrs. D. E. Barnes, Marietta, Georgia

TINY PARTY TASSIES

1 3-oz. package cream cheese	2 eggs, beaten
1 c. butter or margarine	1 tsp. vanilla
1 c. flour	1 c. seedless raisins
1 c. sugar	1 c. chopped nuts

Blend the cream cheese and 1/2 cup butter in a bowl, then stir in the flour. Chill for 1 hour or longer. Mix remaining butter, sugar, eggs, vanilla, raisins and nuts in a bowl. Shape dough into small balls and press into miniature muffin cups. Spoon rounded teaspoon of filling into each crust. Bake at 325 degrees for 25 to 30 minutes.

Mrs. H. L. Josey, Savannah, Georgia

TINY TAFFY TASSIES

1 recipe pie pastry	1 egg, beaten
Chopped pecans or walnuts	1 c. (packed) brown sugar

2 tbsp. milk	1/4 tsp. salt
1/4 c. melted butter	1 tsp. vanilla

Line miniature muffin cups with pie crust. Add 1 teaspoon pecans to each cup. Mix the egg, brown sugar, milk, butter, salt and vanilla and fill each cup 2/3 full. Bake at 350 degrees for 30 minutes.

Joyce Martin, Long Beach, California

STRAWBERRY MOCHA TARTLETS

4 c. sifted all-purpose flour	1/2 c. sugar
2 tsp. salt	6 egg yolks
1 1/2 c. vegetable shortening	1 tbsp. instant coffee powder
2 pt. fresh strawberries	2 tbsp. cocoa
Light corn syrup	1 c. softened sweet butter
1/2 c. strong coffee	

Combine the flour and salt in bowl. Cut in the shortening until uniform but coarse. Sprinkle with 1/2 cup water and toss with fork, then press into ball. Roll out 1/2 of the dough at a time on a lightly floured surface to a 1/8-inch thickness. Cut into 3-inch circles, then fit inside 2 1/4-inch tart pans and prick with fork. Place on a baking sheet. Bake in a 425-degree oven for 10 minutes or until lightly browned. Cool and remove from tart pans. Brush the strawberries with corn syrup and let dry on racks. Combine the coffee and sugar and boil to the thread stage or until candy thermometer registers 234 degrees. Beat the egg yolks with the instant coffee powder and cocoa until fluffy and thick. Add the hot syrup gradually to yolks, pouring in a thin steady stream and beating constantly. Continue beating until light in color and cold, then beat in butter. Chill slightly if necessary. Pipe a ring of the butter mixture around the inside edge of each cooled tartlet shell. Place a strawberry in each shell and chill until served. 50 servings.

gourmet patisserie

A shop that features the pastries sought by gourmets — that's what you have in this section. The delightful, home-tested recipes here are prefaced by informative material written especially to help you become a gourmet pastry-maker. The recipes themselves are the time-proven favorites of women who have earned a reputation as great pastry-makers, women of the Southland. These are recipes with all the uncertainty long since cooked out, leaving only easy to follow directions certain to bring you success.

When nothing but the best will do for dessert, think torte! These light and airy desserts have been favorites in gourmet pastry shops for years — and they are yours to serve with the recipes you'll find for Venetian Cream Torte . . . Chocolate Pecan Torte . . . and more.

You'll also want to experiment with an elegant Souffle Cheesecake . . . Almond Macaroon . . . Peach Meringue . . . and Cherry Strudel. These are the queens of the pastry world, the pastries that only the best pastry-makers can prepare.

Join that select group now, by preparing some of the recipes you'll find in this unusual section. Once you discover how easy gourmet pastry-making is, you'll wonder that you didn't try it before. And once you hear those almost-envious compliments from your friends, you'll be glad that you, too, became a gourmet pastry-maker!

The concept of a *gourmet patisserie*, a bake shop featuring pastries of a particularly delicate and rich nature, is at least 500 years old. In the late 1400's, such shops had their beginnings when an enterprising Viennese baker sold rolls stamped with the Austro-Hungarian emperor's profile. The demand for these delicious white rolls was followed by a demand for other bakery products — and the varied and exquisite pastries characteristic of Austria and Hungary were born.

In the strictest sense of the word, these delicacies are not pastries at all. Rather, they are very rich, extremely sweet foods with a flaky texture often associated with the very finest pies and pastries. Perhaps that is why over the years these foods, more than any others, have been grouped together as features of the gourmet patisserie. In assembling the recipes that follow, we have chosen foods typical of those found in the very best patisseries.

gourmet skills
FOR PIES AND PASTRIES

Even today, when people are more calorie conscious than in times past, gourmet patisseries thrive. Such bake shops feature cheesecake, tortes (cloud-like cakes in which nuts and bread crumbs replace the flour), eclairs, napoleons, josephines, strudel, and other sweet-tooth pleasers. In Europe, there are long-standing feuds between patisseries over which has the best foods. All the finest patisseries pride themselves on searching out the finest ingredients and in using the creative genius of great pastry chefs to produce breathtaking confections that delight the eye as well as the palate.

BECOMING A GOURMET PATISSIER

To become a gourmet patissier — a gourmet-pleasing pastry-maker — is to master an intricate art. And its mastery brings a feeling of excitement that makes cooking a true adventure. That mastery comes from an attention to preparation, a seeking for the finest foods, and a sense of innovation that can transform local ingredients into delicious treats.

In addition to such attributes, a gourmet patissier learns about the foods being prepared. As you browse through these pages, you will encounter recipes for *cheesecake*. In preparing it, remember that cheesecake must never be handled too much or too heavily. A springform pan, an inexpensive utensil available at many stores, will enable you to bake the cake and take it from the pan without ever once turning it over or otherwise jarring it and causing it to fall. Remember, too, that cheesecake is baked at a very low temperature. The low temperature is important because eggs and cheese, two of the principal ingredients in cheesecake, toughen at high temperatures.

Another delicacy you will encounter in this section is *tortes*, the light cakes often topped with whipped cream, jams, chocolate, or other sweets. Like cheesecake, tortes are delicate and should be handled as little as possible. A springform pan will help protect the fragile texture of these cakes. When preparing a torte, remember that finely ground nuts and bread crumbs often replace the flour. The nuts should be light, dry, and flaky. An ordinary food grinder will reduce nuts to a sodden paste. If you invest in an inexpensive hand nut grinder, it will pay rich dividends. These grinders are specially designed to yield the flaky nut particles so essential to creating a light torte. Tortes are a kind of sponge cake and like sponge cakes, they rise through the clinging of the cake batter to the ungreased sides of a pan. The pans for these cakes should never be greased.

Still another pastry featured in gourmet patisseries and in this section is *strudel*. This flaky pastry is a descendent of the Middle Eastern *baklava*, a dessert made of thin, flaky pastry layers filled with chopped nuts, honey, or other ingredients. Baklava was long a favorite dessert of the Turks and Greeks. Their neighbors, the Hungarians borrowed it, gave it a filling of chopped nuts and/or fruit, and christened it *strudel*. Even today, strudel is a popular pastry in Austria, Hungary, Germany, and in the United States. Strudel making is a difficult art, but it has been simplified by the introduction of new flours that enable a cook to create the paper-thin strudel dough with a minimum of fuss.

Cheesecake, tortes, and strudel are just three of the pastries you will discover in this section. Here, too, you will find recipes for *macaroons*, a confection whose flavor and texture mingle in an indescribably delicious combination. This chapter is one that is certain to bring a sense of adventure to your cooking — and delicious enjoyment to your family and friends!

WALPURGIS NIGHT CAKE

2 1/8 c. flour	7/8 c. margarine
6 1/2 tbsp. sugar	1 egg

Combine all the ingredients in a bowl and mix well, then knead until smooth. Refrigerate for 1 hour or longer. Divide dough into 3 parts, then roll out into 9-inch circles. Place on greased baking sheets. Bake at 425 degrees for about 10 minutes or until lightly browned. Cool.

Cake

3 eggs, separated	5/8 c. flour
5/8 c. sugar	1/2 tsp. baking powder

Beat the egg whites until stiff peaks form, then fold in the beaten egg yolks and sugar. Combine the flour and baking powder and fold into the egg mixture. Turn into a greased 9-inch cake pan. Bake at 350 degrees for about 25 minutes or until cake tests done. Cool on rack, then split in half, crosswise.

Filling

4 egg yolks, lightly beaten	1 tsp. vanilla
5 1/2 tbsp. butter	1 1/4 c. raspberry jam
1/4 c. sugar	1 pkg. slivered almonds, toasted
1 1/4 c. whipping cream	

Combine the egg yolks, butter, sugar and cream in a heavy saucepan. Simmer, stirring constantly, until thickened. Remove from heat and beat until cool, then stir in the vanilla. Place a pastry layer on serving dish and spread with 1/3 of the jam. Cover with a cake layer and spread with 1/2 of the filling. Add a pastry layer and spread with 1/3 of the jam. Cover with the remaining cake layer and remaining filling. Top with remaining pastry layer and remaining jam. Sprinkle with the almonds. Refrigerate overnight.

Photograph for this recipe on page 171.

CARAMEL-YAM TORTE

4 egg whites	1 1/2 c. chopped nuts
1/2 tsp. cream of tartar	1/2 c. buttery round cracker
1/2 c. sugar	crumbs
1/2 tsp. cinnamon	1 c. mashed cooked yams
1/4 tsp. nutmeg	20 caramels
1/4 tsp. cloves	1/2 c. cream
1 tsp. vanilla	1 c. whipped cream

Beat the egg whites with cream of tartar in a mixing bowl until stiff peaks form. Beat in sugar gradually and beat in spices and vanilla. Fold in 1 cup nuts, cracker crumbs and yams and turn into 2 well-greased 8-inch cake pans. Bake at 350 degrees for 30 minutes. Cool and remove from pans. Combine caramels and cream in a saucepan and cook over low heat, stirring occasionally, until caramels are melted and mixture is smooth. Place 1 torte layer on a serving plate and pour half the caramel sauce over torte. Top with remaining nuts. Add remaining torte layer and cover with remaining caramel sauce. Top with whipped cream.

Wanda Taylor, Grayson, Louisiana

VIENNESE WALNUT-MOCHA TORTE

1 pkg. yellow cake mix	1/2 c. chopped walnuts
1/4 tsp. salt	1 pkg. chocolate pudding mix
3 egg whites	1 c. strong coffee
3/4 c. sugar	1 c. milk

Prepare the cake mix according to package directions and pour into 2 greased and floured 9-inch round cake pans. Place salt and egg whites in a bowl and beat until frothy. Add sugar gradually, beating well after each addition, and beat until stiff. Spread over cake batter and sprinkle walnuts over meringue. Bake at 325 degrees for about 30 minutes. Cool cake for 5 minutes and loosen meringue from sides of pans. Let stand for about 10 minutes longer, then turn onto wire rack. Turn right side up immediately and cool. Split each layer in half. Prepare pudding mix according to package directions, using coffee and milk for liquid, and chill. Spread on cake layers and place layers together, beginning and ending with meringue layers. Refrigerate until chilled. 12 servings.

Mrs. Charles H. Howe, Jr., Takoma Park, Maryland

ALMOND-VANILLA TORTE

3/4 c. butter or margarine	5 tbsp. flour
5/8 c. sugar	1 1/4 c. whipping cream
5/8 c. finely chopped almonds	1/2 tsp. vanilla
1 tbsp. cream	1/4 c. confectioners' sugar

Combine the butter and sugar, then cream until fluffy. Stir in the almonds, cream and flour. Spread 1/4 of the batter thin to the edge of a large pancake griddle. Bake at 425 degrees until brown, then cool and turn out on a flat surface. Repeat with the remaining batter. Beat the cream until soft peaks form, then add the vanilla and confectioners' sugar gradually and beat until stiff peaks form. Spread the the cream mixture between the thin cake layers.

VENETIAN CREME TORTE

1/2 c. margarine	1/2 c. cocoa
1 2/3 c. sugar	1/2 tsp. soda
3 eggs	1/4 tsp. salt
1 tsp. vanilla	1 c. buttermilk
2 c. cake flour	

Cream the margarine and sugar in a bowl until light and fluffy. Add the eggs, one at a time, beating well after each addition, and blend in vanilla. Sift the flour, cocoa, soda and salt together and add to creamed mixture alternately with buttermilk. Pour into 3 greased and floured 9-inch round cake pans. Bake at 350 degrees for 18 to 20 minutes. Place pans on wire rack and cool. Remove from pans and cut each layer in half, making 6 layers.

Buttercream Filling

1/2 c. sugar	1 c. butter
1/2 c. flour	1 1/2 c. confectioners' sugar
1/2 tsp. salt	1 tsp. vanilla
2 2/3 c. milk	

Combine the sugar, flour and salt in a saucepan and add milk gradually. Bring to a boil over low heat, stirring constantly. Cook for 5 minutes then chill. Cream the butter until light and fluffy and add 3/4 cup confectioners' sugar gradually. Add chilled mixture alternately with remaining confectioners' sugar. Add vanilla and beat until smooth. Spread between layers and on top of torte. 12-16 servings.

Mrs. Bob Hines, Mt. Olive, North Carolina

BLITZ TORTE WITH RICH CUSTARD FILLING

1/2 c. soft shortening	3 tbsp. milk
1 1/4 c. sifted confectioners' sugar	1 1/8 c. sugar
	1/2 c. slivered blanched almonds
6 eggs	2 c. light cream
1 3/8 c. sifted flour	2 tsp. vanilla
1 tsp. baking powder	Sweetened whipped cream (opt.)
3/4 tsp. salt	

Cream the shortening and 3/4 cup confectioners' sugar in a mixing bowl and beat in 4 egg yolks. Sift 1 cup flour, baking powder and 1/4 teaspoon salt together and blend into egg yolk mixture. Stir in milk and spread in 2 greased and floured 8-inch round cake pans. Beat 4 egg whites until frothy and beat in remaining confectioners' sugar and 1/2 cup sugar gradually. Beat until stiff and spread over batter in cake pans. Sprinkle with 2 tablespoons sugar and almonds. Bake at 325 degrees for 35 to 40 minutes and cool. Mix remaining sugar, salt and flour in a saucepan and stir in the cream. Bring to a boil over low heat, stirring, and boil for 1 minute. Beat remaining eggs and stir small amount of cream mixture into eggs. Stir back into cream mixture and bring to a boil. Remove from heat and cool. Stir in vanilla. Spread over meringue side of cake layers and stack layers, custard side up. Place whipped cream in a pastry bag and pipe over torte. 12 servings.

Mrs. Frank Meigs, Montgomery, Alabama

SCOTCH ALMOND PIZZA

1 c. almond paste	2 tbsp. cake flour
7/8 c. sugar	Dash of salt
3 egg whites, lightly beaten	Pineapple pie filling
1/2 tsp. vanilla	Large maraschino cherries
1/3 c. confectioners' sugar	Large green grapes

Crumble the almond paste into small pieces in a bowl, then add the sugar and mix until well blended. Mix in the egg whites and vanilla. Sift the confectioners' sugar, flour and salt together, then stir into the egg white mixture. Spread half the mixture in a 9-inch square on a foil-lined cookie sheet. Pipe the remaining mixture through a pastry tube across the top and around edge to form 9 squares. Let stand, covered, for 2 hours or longer. Bake in preheated 300-degree oven for 25 minutes or until lightly browned. Cool thoroughly. Spread a thin layer of pie filling in each square and arrange the cherries in 5 squares and grapes in the remaining squares.

HEAVENLY PIZZA

2 3/4 c. flour	2 c. fresh whole blueberries
1 tsp. salt	1/2 c. cinnamon
3/4 c. shortening	1/4 tsp. nutmeg
6 tbsp. cold water	1/2 c. butter
2 c. sliced nectarines	

Combine 2 cups flour and salt in a bowl, then cut in the shortening. Stir in the water and mix well. Turn onto a floured board and roll pastry into a 15-inch circle, trimming circle edge with pastry wheel. Place the pastry on a pizza pan. Arrange the fruits evenly over the pastry. Combine the remaining flour, cinnamon and nutmeg and cut in the butter until crumbly. Sprinkle over the fruits. Turn up the pastry edge. Bake at 450 degrees for 20 to 30 minutes or until fruit is tender and crust and topping are golden brown. Cut into wedges to serve.

Mrs. Lenora Waites, Fairmont, West Virginia

SUMMER BASKET WITH STRAWBERRIES

4 egg whites	1/4 tsp. vanilla
1 1/4 c. confectioners' sugar	3 tbsp. sugar
3/4 c. whipping cream	1 qt. whole strawberries

Preheat the oven to 225 degrees. Beat the egg whites until foamy, then add the confectioners' sugar gradually, beating until stiff peaks form. Draw two 6 1/2-inch circles on brown paper, then grease the circles well. Place paper on baking sheet. Place the meringue in a pastry tube. Force the meringue through the tube

to fill 1 circle for bottom of basket. Begin to fill the circle from the outside and move toward the center in a spiral movement until the circle is completely covered. Form a thick ring on the outline of the remaining drawn circle. Do not fill in. Draw 2 more circles on another sheet of paper, then grease the circles and place the paper on another baking sheet. Force the meringue through tube around the edge of the circles to form thick rims. Reserve the remaining meringue for filling. Place 1 sheet on lower rack of oven and remaining sheet on higher rack. Bake for 20 minutes, then reverse sheets on racks and bake for 25 minutes longer. Cover with foil if meringue browns too fast. Remove from oven and loosen the meringues from paper, then place the papers on cooling racks. Place the solid-filled meringue layer on an ovenproof platter. Spread with part of the reserved meringue, then add the rings, spreading the meringue between each ring to hold basket together. Return to the oven and bake for about 5 to 10 minutes longer. Whip the cream until soft peaks form, then add the vanilla and sugar gradually, beating until stiff peaks form. Arrange the strawberries and whipped cream in alternate layers in the basket.

ANGEL-CHOCOLATE MERINGUE

2 egg whites	1 1/2 tsp. vanilla
1/8 tsp. salt	1/4 lb. sweet cooking
1/8 tsp. cream of tartar	chocolate
1/2 c. sugar	3 tbsp. water
1/2 c. chopped walnuts or	1 c. whipped cream, whipped
pecans	

Combine the egg whites, salt and cream of tartar and beat until foamy. Add the sugar, 2 tablespoons at a time, beating until well blended, then beat until stiff peaks form. Fold in the walnuts and 1/2 teaspoon vanilla. Spoon into a lightly greased 8-inch pie pan, shaping into a nest-like shell and building sides up to 1/2-inch above edge of pan. Bake at 300 degrees for 50 to 55 minutes. Combine the chocolate and water in a saucepan and melt over low heat, then cool. Add the remaining vanilla. Fold the chocolate mixture into the whipped cream. Fill the shell and chill for 2 hours or longer.

Mrs. Charles F. White, Memphis, Tennessee

CHOCOLATE-TOFFEE MERINGUE

7 egg whites	1 pt. heavy cream
1 3/4 c. sugar	Vanilla to taste
9 cold chocolate-toffee bars	

Beat the egg whites in a large bowl until frothy. Add the sugar, small amount at a time, beating constantly until stiff. Place on 2 well-greased and waxed paper-lined cake pans. Bake at 300 degrees for 1 hour. Crush the toffee bars. Whip the heavy cream until stiff, adding vanilla and additional sugar to taste. Place 1 meringue on cake plate and cover with half the whipped cream. Sprinkle with half the candy crumbs. Place remaining meringue on candy crumbs and cover with remaining whipped cream. Sprinkle with remaining candy crumbs. Refrigerate for 10 hours before serving. 12 servings.

Mrs. Gavin G. Craig, Jr., Alvaton, Kentucky

COFFEE CLOUDS

3 egg whites	Dash of salt
1 tsp. vanilla	1 c. sugar
1/4 tsp. cream of tartar	1 tsp. instant coffee

Combine first 4 ingredients in a mixing bowl and beat till frothy. Mix sugar and coffee and add to egg white mixture gradually. Beat till stiff peaks form. Shape into 8 circles on brown paper-lined baking sheets. Bake at 450 degrees for 15 minutes or until lightly browned.

Filling

1 6-oz. package butterscotch pieces	Dash of salt
3 tbsp. water	1 egg, beaten
1 tbsp. instant coffee	1 c. heavy cream, whipped

Combine the butterscotch pieces, water, coffee and salt in a saucepan and cook and stir over low heat till butterscotch pieces melt. Cook for 2 minutes longer. Stir small amount into egg, then return to butterscotch mixture. Cook for 1 minute, stirring constantly, and remove from heat. Chill for several hours. Spread over meringues; top with whipped cream.

Mrs. June R. Meinberg, North Miami Beach, Florida

GEORGIA CRACKER-NUT MERINGUE

20 saltine crackers	1 1/3 c. sugar
1 1/4 tsp. baking powder	1 tsp. vanilla
4 egg whites	1 c. chopped pecans

Crush the crackers into fine crumbs, then mix in the baking powder. Beat the egg whites until stiff, but not dry. Beat in the sugar gradually, beating until stiff. Fold in the vanilla, pecans and crumbs, mixing well but gently. Pour into a well-greased 9-inch pie pan. Bake at 350 degrees for 30 minutes or until golden brown and firm. Let cool. Garnish pie with dessert topping and sliced fruit, if desired.

Mrs. Julian A. Grantham, Cochran, Georgia

PEACH MERINGUE

3 egg whites	1/2 c. chopped pecans
1 c. sugar	1 tsp. vanilla
12 soda crackers, rolled fine	1/2 pt. whipping cream
1/4 tsp. baking powder	2 c. sliced drained peaches

Beat the egg whites until stiff adding 3/4 cup sugar gradually. Combine the crumbs, baking powder and pecans. Add to the egg whites, then add the vanilla and fold together gently. Turn into a buttered pie plate, shaping up the side. Bake at 325 degrees for 30 minutes. Cool thoroughly. Whip the cream until thick and add the remaining sugar. Fold in the peaches and pour over the baked crust, then spread to edge. Chill for 12 hours.

Mrs. Jack L. Adams, Richmond, Kentucky

LIME PRINCESS MERINGUE

3 eggs, separated	1/4 c. lime juice
1/4 tsp. cream of tartar	1 1/2 tsp. grated lime rind
1/8 tsp. salt	1 c. heavy cream, whipped
1 c. sugar	

Beat the egg whites until foamy, then add the cream of tartar and salt and beat until stiff, but not dry. Add 3/4 cup sugar gradually, beating until very stiff. Cover the baking sheet with heavy brown paper. Mark a circle, 8 inches in diameter, on the paper. Cover the circle with the meringue, about 1/2-inch deep. Spoon meringue around edge of circle forming a rim. Bake at 275 degrees for 1 hour. Leave on paper to cool. Beat the egg yolks lightly in the top of a double boiler, then add the remaining sugar and the lime juice and beat until well blended. Cook over boiling water, stirring constantly until thickened. Add the lime rind. Remove from heat and chill. Fold into the whipped cream. Place the meringue on a scrving plate, and fill with the cream mixture. Chill for at least 6 hours. Garnish with lime slices, mint leaves or cherries, if desired. 6 servings.

Mrs. Eudora D. Monk, Kerrville, Texas

HEAVENLY MERINGUE VACHERIN

4 egg whites	1 c. sugar
1/2 tsp. cream of tartar	1/2 tsp. vanilla
1/8 tsp. salt	

Beat the egg whites with the cream of tartar and salt until soft peaks form, then add the sugar gradually, beating until stiff. Fold in the vanilla. Turn into a 9-inch pie pan. Bake in a 275-degree oven for 1 hour. Cool thoroughly.

Filling

4 egg yolks	1/4 c. crushed pineapple
Sugar	with syrup
Dash of salt	3/4 c. whipping cream
Grated lemon rind	1/2 c. grated coconut
2 tbsp. lemon juice	

Combine the egg yolks, 1/2 cup sugar, salt, lemon rind and juice with the pineapple and syrup in a double boiler. Cook over hot water, stirring, until thick. Cool thoroughly. Spread over the meringue crust. Whip the cream with 2 tablespoons sugar and spread over the pineapple mixture. Sprinkle with coconut. Chill for 12 hours before serving.

Mrs. Bruce Wallace, Asheville, North Carolina

MERINGUE HEARTS WITH STRAWBERRY ICE CREAM

3 egg whites
Dash of salt
1/2 tsp. vinegar
1/4 tsp. vanilla

1 c. sugar
1/2 gal. strawberry ice
cream

Place the egg whites in a small, deep mixing bowl. Add the salt, vinegar and vanilla and beat with electric mixer at high speed until stiff peaks form. Add sugar gradually and beat until very stiff. Place 6 mounds of egg white mixture on a cookie sheet covered with brown paper. Form each mound into a heart shell with the back of a teaspoon. Bake in 300-degree oven for 45 minutes. Remove from paper immediately and cool. Fill meringue hearts with ice cream and serve immediately.

Darlene Hicks, Atlanta, Texas

PECAN MERINGUE

3 egg whites
1 c. graham cracker crumbs
1 c. sugar

1/2 tsp. baking powder
1 c. chopped nuts

Beat the egg whites until stiff. Mix the remaining ingredients together and fold into the egg whites. Turn into a buttered pie pan. Bake at 325 degrees for 30 minutes. Cool. Garnish with whipped cream if desired.

Mrs. Cecil Shields, La Blanca, Texas

MYSTERY MERINGUE

16 sm. buttery cookies,
crumbled
2/3 c. chopped pecans
1/2 tsp. baking powder

1 c. sugar
3 egg whites
1 tsp. vanilla

Whirl the crumbs and pecans in a blender until quite fine. Sift the baking powder and sugar together. Beat the egg whites until stiff, adding the sugar mixture gradually. Fold in the crumb mixture when whites are almost stiff, then add the vanilla. Pour into a lightly greased 8-inch square pan. Bake in 350-degree oven for 30 minutes. Cool.

1/2 pt. whipping cream
2 tbsp. sugar

Grated sweet cooking
chocolate

Whip the cream until stiff, then beat in the sugar. Spread over cooled meringue. Garnish with chocolate shavings. Refrigerate for at least 3 hours. Cut into squares before serving.

J. S. Davis, Jacksonville, Florida

DUTCH APPLE TREAT

2 tbsp. butter
1/2 c. sifted flour
1/2 c. milk

3 eggs
1/2 tsp. salt

Melt the butter in a 9-inch skillet over low heat and combine the flour, milk, eggs and salt in mixing bowl. Tilt the skillet so sides are coated with butter and pour all remaining butter into the bowl. Beat with a rotary beater until smooth and pour into the buttered skillet. Bake at 425 degrees for 20 minutes. Reduce oven temperature to 350 degrees and bake for 15 minutes longer.

Poached Golden Apple Slices

4 Washington State golden
    Delicious apples
3/4 c. sugar
3/4 c. water

3 tbsp. lemon juice
4 whole cloves
Dash of salt
2 tbsp. butter

Pare, core and cut the apples into eighths. Combine the sugar, water, lemon juice, cloves and salt in a large skillet and bring to a boil. Add the apples and simmer, covered, for 5 minutes. Remove cover and cook for 3 to 5 minutes longer or until apples are cooked through and glazed, turning apples frequently and spooning syrup over top. Discard the cloves. Spoon the apples into hot baked shell. Add the butter to the syrup remaining in the skillet and heat, stirring until butter is melted, then spoon over the apples. Cut into wedges to serve.

WENATCHEE APPLE BRAID

3 Washington State Jonathan apples	2 tbsp. (packed) brown sugar
1/4 c. water	1 tbsp. melted butter
1/2 c. diced dried apricots	2 tsp. shredded lemon peel
6 tbsp. broken walnuts	1 tsp. cinnamon
	Pastry for 2-crust pie

Pare, core and quarter the apples. Place in a saucepan with the water and cook until tender. Drain and mash to 1 cup of sauce. Mix the applesauce, apricots, walnuts, brown sugar, melted butter, lemon peel and cinnamon together. Roll out pastry to a 14 x 8-inch rectangle. Spoon the apple mixture down center of pastry, then cut the pastry with scissors, 2 1/2 inches from both sides at 1-inch intervals. Fold strips across top of filling, alternating left and right. Moisten strips to secure at overlap point. Slip onto cookie sheet. Bake at 425 degrees for about 35 minutes or until pastry is done and golden brown. May sprinkle with cinnamon sugar or dribble with a light glaze, if desired.

PEANUT MACCOTTE

1 6 1/2-oz. box fluffy white frosting mix	1 tsp. vanilla
1 c. crushed cinnamon graham cracker crumbs	1 c. chopped peanuts
	Whipped cream

Prepare the frosting mix according to package directions, then fold in the crumbs, vanilla and peanuts. Pile lightly in a buttered 9-inch pie pan. Bake at 350 degrees for about 30 minutes. Cut in wedges and serve warm with whipped cream.

Mrs. Estell Shalla, Bay City, Texas

APRICOT STRUDEL

1 c. soft butter	1 c. chopped pecans
1 8-oz. package cream	1 lb. golden raisins
cheese, softened	1 4-oz. package shredded
2 c. sifted flour	coconut
2 c. apricot preserves	

Cream the butter and cream cheese thoroughly, then blend in the flour, mixing until dough forms ball. Chill for 3 to 4 hours. Divide the dough into 3 equal parts, then roll each to a 14 x 16-inch rectangle on a floured surface. Spread the preserves over dough, being careful not to tear, then sprinkle with the pecans, raisins and coconut. Roll each as for jelly roll and place on ungreased baking sheets. Bake at 350 degrees for 45 minutes. Slice to serve.

Sandra Kay Ehlers Park, Baytown, Texas

APRICOT STRUDLETS

1 c. sour cream	1 can flaked coconut
1/2 lb. margarine	Coarsely chopped nuts
2 c. flour	to taste
1 lge. jar apricot preserves	Confectioners' sugar

Combine the sour cream and margarine and blend until smooth, then add the flour, mixing well. Divide into 5 parts and chill overnight. Combine the preserves and coconut. Roll each part of dough out thin and spread with the preserves mixture. Sprinkle generously with nuts and roll up jelly roll fashion. Place on ungreased baking sheet. Slice 3/4 the way through roll at 1-inch intervals. Bake at 350 degrees for about 35 minutes. Remove from oven and cut all the way through, then roll each in confectioners' sugar.

Mrs. Evelyn Smith, Tampa, Florida

CHERRY STREUSEL

2 1/2 c. flour	2 sticks butter
2 tsp. baking powder	1 tsp. vanilla
1 tsp. cinnamon	1 1-lb. can sweet
1 c. sugar	cherries
1 egg	1 1-lb. can tart cherries

Combine the flour, baking powder and cinnamon in a mixing bowl, then hollow out the center and place the sugar in the middle. Place the egg over the sugar, then mix with the sugar and blend in the flour mixture. Cut the butter into small pieces and mix in until thoroughly blended. Knead by hand until thoroughly mixed. Add the vanilla. Divide the dough into 2 equal parts, then flatten 1 part into bottom of 9-inch springform pan. Drain the cherries and arrange the cherries over the dough. Crumble remaining dough over the cherries. Bake at 350 degrees for 1 hour. 8-10 servings.

Nancy O'Connor Haukohl, Huntsville, Alabama

CHEESECAKE SUPREME

1 c. sifted all-purpose flour	1/2 c. butter or margarine
1/4 c. sugar	1 egg yolk, slightly beaten
1 tsp. grated lemon peel	1/4 tsp. vanilla

Combine the flour, sugar and lemon peel in a bowl and cut in butter until mixture is consistency of meal. Add the egg yolk and vanilla and blend thoroughly. Pat 1/3 of the mixture on bottom of 9-inch springform pan with sides removed. Bake at 400 degrees for 8 minutes or until golden. Cool. Attach sides of pan to bottom and pat remaining dough on sides to height of 1 3/4 inches.

Filling

5 8-oz. packages cream cheese	1/4 tsp. salt
1/4 tsp. vanilla	4 eggs
3/4 tsp. grated lemon peel	2 egg yolks
1 3/4 c. sugar	1/4 c. whipping cream
3 tbsp. all-purpose flour	

Place the cream cheese in a bowl and let stand at room temperature until soft. Beat until creamy. Add the vanilla and lemon peel and mix. Mix the sugar, flour and salt and add to cream cheese mixture gradually. Add the eggs and egg yolks, one at a time, beating after each addition just until blended. Stir in the whipping cream, then pour into crust-lined pan. Bake at 450 degrees for 12 minutes. Reduce temperature to 300 degrees and bake for 55 minutes longer. Remove from oven and cool for 30 minutes. Loosen sides with spatula. Cool for 30 minutes and remove from pan. Cool for 2 hours longer.

Strawberry Glaze

3 c. strawberries	2 tbsp. cornstarch
1 c. water	1/2 to 3/4 c. sugar

Crush the strawberries in a saucepan. Add the water and cook for 2 minutes. Press through a sieve and place the puree back in the saucepan. Mix the cornstarch with sugar and stir into strawberry puree. Bring to boiling point, stirring constantly. Cook and stir until thick and clear. Cool to room temperature, then pour on the cheesecake. 12 servings.

Mrs. Sarah J. Hightower, Fort Worth, Texas

PINEAPPLE-MINT SURPRISE

1 c. flour	1 pkg. lime gelatin
1/2 c. walnuts, chopped	1 8-oz. package cream cheese
1/4 c. (packed) brown sugar	1 c. sugar
1/2 c. butter	2/3 c. evaporated milk
1 1-lb. 4-oz. can crushed pineapple	1/8 tsp. peppermint extract

Combine the flour, walnuts and brown sugar, then cut in the butter. Press into the bottom of a springform pan. Bake at 400 degrees for 10 minutes, then cool thoroughly. Drain the pineapple and reserve the juice. Pour the reserved juice in a saucepan and bring to a boil, then add the gelatin and stir until dissolved. Cool. Blend the cream cheese with the sugar, then mix into the gelatin and stir in the pineapple. Chill until thickened. Chill the evaporated milk with the peppermint extract in a small bowl until crystals form around edge, then beat until thick. Fold into the pineapple mixture and spoon over the crust. Chill until firm.

Glaze

1/2 c. chocolate chips	1 tsp. butter
1/3 c. evaporated milk	1/4 tsp. peppermint extract

Melt the chocolate chips in milk, then add the butter and extract. Cool slightly, then spread glaze carefully over filling. Chill for 4 hours before serving.

Mrs. Sally Sparkman, London, Kentucky

SNOW CLOUD CHEESECAKE

3 eggs, separated	1 tsp. vanilla
1 8-oz. package cream cheese	1 c. whipping cream, whipped
1 c. sugar	12 graham crackers, crushed
1/2 tsp. salt	

Mix the egg yolks, cream cheese, sugar and salt in a bowl and add vanilla. Fold in stiffly beaten egg whites and whipped cream. Line a mold with half the cracker crumbs and pour the cream cheese mixture over crumbs. Top with remaining crumbs and chill for several hours.

Mrs. W. G. Rohmer, Jr., Mobile, Alabama

SOUFFLE CHEESECAKE

Pastry for 2-crust pie	2 tsp. grated orange rind
6 eggs, separated	1 tbsp. cointreau
1 3/4 c. sugar	2 lb. softened cream cheese
3 tbsp. flour	1 c. cream
3 tbsp. melted butter	

Roll out the pastry on a floured surface and line the bottom and side of a springform pan. Bake in a 450-degree oven for about 15 minutes or until browned. Beat the egg yolks until light. Mix the sugar with flour and add to egg yolks gradually, beating constantly. Add the butter, orange rind and cointreau and beat well. Add the cream cheese and cream and blend until smooth. Fold in the stiffly beaten egg whites and pour into the baked pastry. Bake in 500-degree oven for 10 minutes. Reduce temperature to 225 degrees and bake for about 1 hour longer. Turn off the heat, open oven door and let cake cool in oven. Refrigerate until chilled.

Mrs. Ben Eaton, Brunswick, Georgia

PITA SA ORASIMA

3/4 c. butter	1 tsp. lemon juice
2 c. sugar	2 tbsp. water
Grated peel of 1 lemon	1 tsp. vanilla
1/4 tsp. soda	3/4 c. ground walnuts
7 eggs, separated	3 c. grated Washington State
4 1/3 c. sifted flour	Delicious apples

Cream the butter, then add 1 cup sugar, lemon peel and soda. Mix well, then add the egg yolks and beat well. Add the flour gradually, beating constantly until well blended, then add the lemon juice and water to moisten. Blend thoroughly, then chill. Add the vanilla to the stiffly beaten egg whites. Mix the walnuts and the remaining sugar, then add to the egg whites gradually, beating until very stiff. Fold in the grated apple. Roll out 2/3 of the dough and line sides and bottom of a 9 x 12-inch ungreased baking pan. Cover pastry with the filling. Roll out the remaining dough and cut into thin strips. Arrange lattice fashion over the top. Bake at 250 degrees for about 35 minutes. Increase temperature to 300 degrees and bake for 15 to 20 minutes longer or until light golden brown. Cut into squares to serve.

DANISH PUFF

1 c. flour	2 tbsp. water
1 stick butter or margarine	

Place the flour in a bowl, then cut in the butter until crumbly. Stir in the water with a fork, blending well. Pat onto an ungreased cookie sheet.

Filling

1 stick butter or margarine	2 c. confectioners' sugar
1 c. flour	1 tsp. vanilla
2 tsp. almond extract	2 tbsp. milk
3 eggs	Chopped nuts to taste
1 3-oz. package cream cheese	

Combine 1 cup water and the butter in a saucepan and bring to a boil. Remove from the heat; then add the flour and almond extract and beat until smooth. Add the eggs, one at a time, beating well after each addition. Spread on top of the pastry. Bake at 325 degrees for 50 to 60 minutes. Cool thoroughly. Combine the cream cheese, confectioners' sugar, vanilla and milk in a bowl and beat until smooth. Spread over the cooled pastry, then sprinkle with nuts.

Mrs. Agnes Toler, Birmingham, Alabama

SWISS FRUIT PASTRY ROLL

1 1/2 c. dried pears	Dash of nutmeg
1 1/2 c. dried prunes	Dash of cloves
2 dried figs	2 1/4 c. sifted flour
1 1/2 c. raisins	1/2 tsp. salt
1 c. chopped walnuts	1/2 c. corn oil margarine
1/3 c. sugar	1 egg yolk, slightly beaten
1 tbsp. cinnamon	

Combine the pears, prunes and figs, then cover with water and soak overnight. Drain well. Pit the prunes and force the plumped fruits through a food chopper, using the medium blade. Combine the fruit mixture, raisins, walnuts, sugar, cinnamon, nutmeg and cloves and mix well. Mix flour and salt in mixing bowl, then cut in margarine with a pastry blender or 2 knives until mixture is well mixed and fine crumbs form. Sprinkle 1/4 cup water over the mixture, tossing to blend. Press dough firmly into ball with hands. Roll out between 2 pieces of waxed paper to 16 x 13-inch rectangle, then remove the top piece of waxed paper. Place fruit mixture lengthwise down center of dough, about 2 1/2 inches from ends. Moisten edges of dough with water, then fold sides around fruit mixture, sealing together on top. Fold up ends and seal. Roll over onto ungreased baking sheet so center seam is down. Prick with a fork and brush with the egg yolk. Bake at 375 degrees for about 1 hour or until golden brown. Cool and slice.

PETIT CHOUX WITH ICE CREAM

2 1/2 tbsp. margarine	Vanilla ice cream
1/4 c. flour	Chocolate sauce
1 egg	

Preheat the oven to 425 degrees. Combine 1/4 cup water and the margarine in a saucepan and bring to a boil. Add the flour and beat vigorously until mixture is thick and smooth and comes away from side of pan. Remove from heat and add the egg, beating until smooth. Drop dough into 6 mounds on cookie sheet. Bake until lightly browned. Cool. Cut puffs in half. Fill with ice cream and drizzle top with sauce just before serving.

DON GALLOWAY'S BANANA-CHEESE PIE

1/4 c. melted butter	3 eggs
Sugar	1/2 tsp. grated lemon peel
1 1/2 c. chocolate cookie	2 tbsp. rum
crumbs	1/2 pt. sour cream
3 bananas	1/2 tsp. vanilla
3 3-oz. packages cream	Lemon juice
cheese	

Combine the butter, 2 tablespoons sugar and crumbs, then press against bottom and side of a 9-inch pie pan. Peel and cut 2 bananas into 1-inch chunks. Combine the bananas, cream cheese, 1/2 cup sugar and eggs in a large mixer bowl, then beat until smooth. Stir in lemon peel and rum, then pour into the crumb-lined pan. Bake at 325 degrees for 30 to 35 minutes. Remove from the oven and cool to room temperature. Mix the sour cream with 2 tablespoons sugar and vanilla. Spoon on top of the pie. Slice the remaining banana and dip in lemon juice, then arrange on top of pie. Garnish top with chocolate curls. Refrigerate until serving time.

INDEX

PHOTOGRAPHY CREDITS: Sunkist Growers; The Pie Filling Institute; American Dairy Association; Apple Pantry: Washington State Apple Commission; United Fresh Fruit and Vegetable Association; Florida Citrus Commission; Knox Gelatine; North American Blueberry Council; Cling Peach Advisory Board; Ocean Spray Cranberries, Inc.; Best Foods: A Division of Corn Products Company, International; Filbert/Hazelnut Institute; National Cherry Growers and Industries Foundation; General Foods Kitchens; Procter & Gamble Company: Crisco Division; California Strawberry Advisory Board; Processed Apples Institute; Evaporated Milk Association; National Dairy Council; Standard Brands Products: Royal Puddings and Gelatins, Fleischmann's Yeast, Fleischmann's Margarine; Carnation Evaporated Milk; Nabisco, Inc.; National Pecan Shellers and Processors Association; Angostura-Wuppermann Corporation; The Nestle Company; McCormick and Company, Inc.; The Borden Company; Kraft Foods Kitchens; California Avocado Advisory Board; Standard Fruit and Steamship Company: Cabana Bananas; DIAMOND Walnut Growers, Inc.; Keith Thomas Company; California Raisin Advisory Board.

Printed in the United States of America.